WHEN LIFE HURTS

ALSO BY BRIAN C. STILLER

A Generation Under Siege
Lifegifts
Critical Options
Don't Let Canada Die by Neglect
Was Canada Ever Christian?
From the Tower of Babel to Parliament Hill

Brian C. Stiller
Following undergraduate and graduate studies
at the University of Toronto, Stiller began his
career in communication and leadership in
Youth for Christ, including serving as president. Then as president of the Evangelical
Fellowship of Canada, a national association of
Protestant churches, he spoke out on a wide
range of issues, both in Ottawa and on national
media. He also hosted "The Stiller Report"
and "Cross Currents," national weekly television programs dealing with critical issues facing
people of faith. He founded and for 14 years
was editor-in-chief of the Canadian national
magazine, *Faith Today*. He currently serves as
president of Tyndale College & Seminary in
Toronto. He has written seven books. He and
his wife Lily live in Newmarket, Ontario. They
have two married children and one grandchild.

WHEN LIFE HURTS

A Three-Fold Path to Healing

BRIAN C. STILLER

To Tim Wilson

Brian C. Stiller

London, 2000

■ HarperCollins*PublishersLtd*

The Bible versions used are *The New International Version* for the
Old Testament and *The Message, The New Testament in Contemporary
English*, by Eugene H. Peterson, for the New Testament, unless
otherwise noted.

Excerpts from *The Will to Meaning* by Viktor E. Frankl,
copyright © 1969 by Viktor E. Frankl; afterword © 1988
by Viktor E. Frankl. Used by permission of Dutton Signet, a division
of Penguin Putnam Inc.

http://www.harpercanada.com

HarperCollins books may be purchased for educational, business, or
sales promotional use. For information please write: Special Markets
Department, HarperCollins Canada, 55 Avenue Road,
Toronto, Ontario, Canada M5R 3L2.

First published in hardcover by HarperCollins in 1999
First trade paper edition

Canadian Cataloguing in Publication Data

Stiller, Brian C.
When life hurts: a three-fold path to healing

ISBN 0-00-200026-1 (bound)
ISBN 0-00-638667-9 (pbk.)

1. Suffering – Religious aspects – Christianity.
2. Christian life.
I. Title.

BV4909.S74 2000   248.8'6   C98-932585-7

00 01 02 03 04 HC 8 7 6 5 4 3 2 1

Printed and bound in the United States

CONTENTS

To David and Evelyn Stiller,
who out of their own hurt, share their story
so others too will find the path of healing.

❖

ACKNOWLEDGEMENTS

Writing this book comes by way of gentle insistence from Don Loney of HarperCollins. It was originally his idea, and when I didn't think I had the goods to deliver, it was his vision and encouragement that got me on the way.

As well, I want to express my thanks to Lorna Dueck and Sandy Reynolds for their help in research, to Krysia Lear for her assistance in research and editing, to Dr. Brian Cunnington for his helpful observations and especially to Audrey Dorsch for her work in bridging ideas, filling gaps, shortening lengthy passages and restructuring material. And, finally, my thanks to Ruth Whitt for her enormous help and care in the entire project.

PREFACE

The question "Why does God allow hurt?" is ancient. Scholars, poets, film writers and novelists have for centuries mined its endless veins. My interest is not to offer solutions but rather to search for ways of healing our pain.

I come to this issue—When Life Hurts—not as one especially trained in the science of psychology. While I have studied this, along with other disciplines, on my academic journey, my interest comes from three decades of working with youth and families and providing spiritual counsel in various public forums.

As a child growing up in the home of a minister who served as a "bishop" responsible for churches in a Canadian prairie province, I watched as our father and mother cared for ministers struggling with the ups and downs of public ministry. The setting was in the 1950s. Money was scarce, distances long and needs critical. When ministers, often with their wives, arrived at our home, seldom would they eat in a restaurant or stay in a hotel: Mom would simply add a few extra place settings and we kids would find other places to sleep. In a community that cared, I learned what it meant for hope, faith and love to be the prime ministrations of healing.

Mom and Dad were not only the best of physicians, they were ahead of their time as mentors and teachers. Long after the dishes had been cleared away, they'd allow us children to sit at the supper table observing these healers-of-the-soul practice their loving rituals. In that setting where hurting ministers needed healing so they could in turn heal, my two sisters, two brothers and I had the best of tutorials. No academic curriculum could match that learning environment.

Not only did I learn something about the process—how it is done—but I learned of the source. There were no simplistic lines of "let's feel good." Our parents had no time for slick, quick fixes. They knew that broken lives need patience, care and a whole bunch of love. It is to Hilmer and Mildred Stiller that I owe my understanding of healing.

In the end, what is written is my responsibility. It has been a valuable time of learning and finding insights into ways which our Creator brings healing to us along the pathways of life.

Brian C. Stiller
March 1999

One

WHAT IS A THREE-FOLD PATH TO HEALING?

Inevitably on the human journey, life hurts.

We obviously don't plan for it, and when hurt comes we aren't prepared to deal with the pain. It all seems so unfair. "The good die young," we murmur and point to those we view as morally inferior yet who seem to get away with no disfigurement or broken dreams. If only the drunken driver had been killed in the accident instead of the innocent driver in the other car; if only the abuser suffered sleepless nights; if only the drug dealer had got AIDS and not the addicted teenager.

As personal as our hurt is, it's universal. A parent in Beirut feels the hurt of his child blown up by a terrorist's bomb as does a parent looking down at the mangled body of her child in Sri Lanka. A jilted lover in a Muslim society knows the same sharp pain of rejection as does a Jew or Christian. The despair engulfing a young mother standing at the grave side of her lover, father of her children, provider and friend is as deep in the mountains of China as it is on windswept plains of the North American prairies. All of us, at some place, at some time, experience hurt—a hurt that is screaming out at the world and at God—a pain-stricken demand to know why.

In our compulsive search for healing, we've developed a booming market of therapeutic sciences, which provide psychological and emotional medicine. Burgeoning in the 1970s, fueled by problems people experienced in their marriages, families and in their vocational and community lives, a plethora of psychological services, self-help groups, yoga classes and mediation retreats have invited us to be healed.

I

As we look for something to quiet our hurt, we employ a wide variety of chemical aids and stimulants. With the advent of tranquilizers, our era, characterized by depression, melancholia and anxiety, found a means of controlling runaway depression. Our nerves are soothed by their wonder-working actions, but we still wake up realizing that, though we've been helped over the threshold of pain, pills won't provide legs for the journey.

Even with these medical and psychological services, we are jolted by the shock of pain. Immobilized and disoriented by the plaguing hurts of our lives, we look for reasons. Why me? How does a God of love allow this to happen? What can I do to end it? Who will help? In the end we search for a couch of solace, a hopeful vision or a path of opportunity to find solutions to life's hurts.

It was Saturday night, around 9:00 p.m. The evening dishes were cleared away and my wife Lily, my daughter Muriel and I were reading when we heard a knock at the door. I was surprised; our cottage is located on a chain of lakes some two hours northeast of Toronto. To find us, you have to know which winding back road to take (this was before a phone line had been strung to the cottages of our lake).

I opened the door to see the owner of the grocery and boat store off Highway 507. Trouble, I remember thinking.

"Hello, Brian. Your nephew Brent called. Something has happened. You are to call your brother David and his wife Evelyn," he said slowly, knowing he was bringing bad news.

I climbed into the car and drove quickly to the highway, found a phone and called. Brent answered. Our conversation began the most painful period of our family's journey.

Returning to the cottage, I told my family the shocking news: our niece Jill had died of carbon-monoxide poisoning, apparently self-inflicted. We later learned that, after a high-school party, she had driven into the garage at home and left the car running; eventually she was overcome by fumes and died.

Waves of grief rolled across our family. They would lift for a few moments when we'd remember a happy and funny moment and laugh—out of our need for relief. Then another wave of sorrow would catch us, and we'd be emotionally swept away. For a week our families were united as we walked side by side in unimaginable heartache.

Why? formed the starting point of each question.

What is it that we didn't do that would have changed the course of her actions? we wondered silently.

Or, was this all just an accident?

And, at eighteen? So unfair. So unnecessary. So cruel.

Not only were Jill's teenage friends asking the question, "Where is my life going?" her parents, uncles, aunts and cousins were as well. The funeral at the church was packed. The procession of cars seemed endless. Listening to the eulogies and sermon, I asked myself, What difference is my life making? Under the crushing sorrow of the death of our beautiful and talented niece, poised on the edge of a promising life, we looked inward at ourselves and then tried to peer outward. Would our wounds ever heal? And if so, how?

But this is not the end of the story. Rather it's the beginning of a narrative, weaving into a story of hope, faith and love.

During my first year in high school I picked up a book about an event called the Holocaust. As I read it, the stories and pictures seemed beyond belief—like a sick hoax. Only after checking out its validity could I actually see that those skinny images with ribs you could count were people. Some years later in Toronto, while rummaging through a hardware bin, I noticed a tattoo on the store owner's arm.

"Were you in a Nazi prison camp?" I asked.

"Yes," he said, "I was in Dachau." Reluctantly and slowly he told me the story of his near death. After month upon month of bare survival, he and some friends escaped, and by an underground network, they fled to Switzerland and eventually made their way to Canada.

Some years later as Lily and I quietly walked inside the enclosure of the Dachau camp on the edge of Munich, I wondered about my hardware-store friend and tried to imagine his days there. I tried to feel his suffering while surviving the unbelievable pain of those dark days in that torturous camp. I tried but couldn't.

When Princess Diana died in a car crash in a Paris tunnel in late August 1997, grief was instant and overwhelming. Not since the death of John F. Kennedy have I seen such widespread mourning. Why did people hurt over her death? Her mourners extended beyond the Commonwealth countries such as Canada and Australia—still linked to the British monarchy—to include a world devastated by her passing. How do we account for such depth of feelings? Then, only days later Mother Teresa—the Albanian nun whose work began in the streets of Calcutta and spread worldwide, the diminutive woman who epitomized the greatest of human symbols of love by her giving—died. Yet her funeral was modestly presented and sparsely viewed in contrast to Princess Diana's.

As one commentator noted, while Princess Diana touched the hurting, Mother Teresa took them home. So why the massive outpouring of grief for this princess who had led a charmed life, had betrayed her marital vows and was masterful in using the media? Yes, people saw her as being unfairly treated by her husband and pushed about by the paparazzi, the scavenger-like media. While many try to ferret out reasons for this massive expression of grief, they fall short of offering a satisfying answer. She had linked her soul with millions, far beyond her own comprehension, I'm sure. But despite a convincing rationale for the depth of feeling, grief it was.

While the hurt of mass killings is more than we can fathom, when we reduce these overpowering collective stories to those of individuals, the cacophony is reduced so we can hear the narrative of loss and sorrow. We don't, however, have to go to the killing fields of Asia or the gas ovens of Europe to encounter suffering. We meet it in our own lives. We hear stories of other people in pain. We discover that no one is immune. We learn that fame, charm or even a life of outstanding goodness cannot defy tragedy. Hurt comes in many ways. Some is beyond what most of us have experienced, but hurt is hurt, no matter what its source.

When a loved one dies, the hurt we feel alerts us to our deep feelings. Pain is triggered by being removed from the one we love, the one with whom we've been closely attached. The greater the attachment, the greater the pain. If a child dies, an entire future is gone, never to be lived. This is in contrast to someone older, about whom we rationalize, "Yes, she's lived a long, good life." Though we feel the loss, at least we feel that the person hasn't been cheated.

There are many kinds of losses, each bringing its own pain. A couple learning that their son has AIDS will have questions arising from a different context than someone reading a note on the kitchen table saying that a spouse has packed up and taken off. There is a difference in the nature of the hurt, but to the respective individuals, there is no difference of degree.

SOURCES OF PAIN

Pain is obvious when we know its source. One day while painting our cottage, the ladder slipped and I fell two stories, breaking seven bones in my right wrist. It hurt, and I knew why it hurt. But when we feel a stomach pain, we may have no idea what it is or its cause.

Such unknowing creates its own kind of pain: anxiety over what it may be adds psychological pain to the physical. When my niece Jill died, I ached in my gut. It was real, like a tight metal band crushing me. Was I being physically crushed? No. But the emotional pain made it feel like I was. The point is that, regardless of its source, emotional hurt is real, not to be dismissed by platitudes such as, "There is no real reason for this. It's just in your head."

Each of us feels pain in our own unique way. I can't describe your pain. We all have our own thresholds in experiencing pain. We know, though, when pain is pushing us over the brink. But what brings hurt to our lives? There are many reasons for it.

DEATH

I recall working in Port au Prince, Haiti, as a volunteer with the Grace Children's Hospital, which specialized in children with tubercular illness. One day I went with Gerard, a staff member, to inform a family that their daughter had died at the hospital. Because she was one of thirteen children, I assumed there would be the normal outpouring of grief, but with so many children, the loss of one child surely wouldn't be that catastrophic. What I saw forced me to rethink my assumptions. We parked the Jeep and picked our way along the sewage-stained street to the child's home, crowded in one of the many shantytowns of that Caribbean city. As we did, Gerard warned me to be ready to leave as soon as the family had been informed of the death.

He knocked on the door. When the parents saw him without their daughter, they knew the news was not good. As gently as he could, he told them that their daughter had passed away that morning. The reaction was instant. There was an outbreak of frenzied, hysterical weeping and anger. It was time for us to leave. We quickly retraced out steps and drove away. As we did, I wondered, Why this outpouring of grief? Then I realized that in such extreme poverty, all that really matters is relationships. When you have few or perhaps no material goods and when just surviving the day takes all the energy you have, life is very precious. When all you have to live for is life itself, death is a thief.

Death is the end; there is no going back. It's final. Unresolved issues lie face up, calling on those who remain to deal with them. All the sorrowing in the world will not change that. And it brings pain, in varying degrees depending on the accompanying realities.

GUILT

It was late at night when the phone rang. Late-night phone calls usually mean trouble. It was. I heard my mother's broken voice and knew it was about Dad. He had been in the hospital with coronary problems for some months. Though Dad and I had a mentoring relationship (in fact, when I think of God, I have this childhood image of God being five foot nine, 190 pounds and bald. That was Dad!), I felt guilt over not giving him enough attention during his final months. My two older brothers were in the medical field, and I assumed they would know best what should be done, so foolishly I let the opportunity of those final months slip away. I still feel the pain of guilt over my failure.

If guilt is not resolved, pain increases. Parents naturally feel guilty if a child takes his or her own life. "What did I not do that I should have done," or "What did I do for which I needed to ask forgiveness?" The unfairness of suicide is that the person who takes his life holds all the cards, as it were. He alone knows the reasons. The ending of one's own life exercises power over those left: they have no means of finding resolution, so throughout life they are forced to live with their regrets.

BROKEN RELATIONSHIPS

Since the untying of marriage bonds by way of divorce has been made easier, there has been an avalanche of broken marriages.

7

Though many marriages should never have begun in the first place, and while some children and spouses are better off by separation, how do we find the means to heal the hurt caused by broken relationships?

FINANCIAL FAILURE

At a recent high-school reunion, a schoolmate told us about her father, a man my brother and I had known from working as teenagers at a grocery store. He was a respected member of his Eastern European community and in his desire to provide for his family the good things of life, he took high risks on horse betting. In the end he lost everything and brought great embarrassment to the entire family. For ten years he worked three jobs to pay off the debt (he refused bankruptcy). The pain was made worse by the anger he took out on his children. Eventually the debts were paid, he was restored to respect in his community and his family found joy and solace, but only after living years of hurt.

INJUSTICE

Guy Paul Morin, a young man who lived just north of our home, was convicted of the murder of a young girl. The police thought they had the case figured out before they had sufficient evidence, and in the end the prosecution constructed the facts to fit its theory. Years later when DNA testing was used, we learned that the accused was not the person responsible—after he'd spent years in prison. What hurt!

Hurt also arises from feeling the injustice done to someone else. Pastor Martin Niemoller and Dietrich Bonhoeffer, who led the Evangelical Church of Germany, stood up to Hitler and his Nazi enterprise. Their deep sense that the church and the German people were being wronged by the demagoguery of the Third Reich, along with their growing awareness of gross violations against the Jewish people, led them to oppose the Führer. Their hurt in seeing the church seduced by the evil of the regime overpowered any fear of personal danger. In the end Niemoller was put behind the barbed wire of the Sachsenhausen concentration camp, and Bonhoeffer was executed.

STRESS

One generally doesn't experience stress from working too hard, but rather as a result of working outside of one's areas of aptitude. I worked with a colleague who was highly skilled in logistics and computers. Because of his competence, he rose in the organization and was eventually made vice president of administration. But his strength was not in dealing with others, and it caused him great stress. He started waking up early in the morning, unable to get a full night's sleep. Pressure built in the organization, conflict rose in his marriage, and in the end he suffered a nervous breakdown. It wasn't that he was overworked, but rather that he was put in charge of an area outside the boundaries of his gifts and expertise.

MORAL FAILURE

This hurt reflects on one's character, and thus is seen as being the worst of all failures. For example, a banker who absconds with funds is viewed as committing a moral failure because he was in a position of trust. A minister caught lying is shocking, for the least one would expect of a minister is that he would uphold in his personal life the character of Jesus. In recent years we have heard about the details of public leaders in all sorts of moral violations. However, it's true that all of us, at some time in our lives, fail morally. Our embarrassment and humiliation are part of the pain, but the hurt of knowing we have caused hurt to others only increases the pain.

NO TIME

Pain comes by not having enough time or by failing to plan. By so doing I bring pain on myself and on others. Too often it's children who suffer. Parents who have little time for their children inflict life-long hurt.

ILLNESS

This brings more than physical hurt and discomfort. It inflicts interior pain on the person who is ill as well as on those who care about him. A colleague of mine who has operated with high energy is now suffering from chronic fatigue syndrome. He doesn't suffer physically, but the impact on his sense of self and family is nothing short of painful.

CHANGE

In *Future Shock* Alvin Toffler describes the social/psychological disease caused by our fast-changing pace of life. In the past we had time to absorb changes, as the time lapse between major shifts allowed the opportunity for people to absorb them. With the rapidity of change today, we are disoriented as change falls close upon change. Computers help build the next generation of computers, so that the time gap from one generation to another is getting shorter and shorter.

MISUNDERSTANDINGS

These hurt. Often they are small and perhaps insignificant, but they annoy us like a pebble in a shoe. These happen as we work with co-workers and live with family. If left unresolved they can become like festering sores, growing until they become debilitating.

UNREALIZED DREAMS

Those of us in middle age are especially vulnerable to a sense of life not being what we had dreamed. As we move through the last few decades of our lives, we wonder if time has passed us by and we've lost the chance to fulfill our dreams. Each of us has that inner hope of writing our signature on some part of the universe, to make our lives count. At a recent high-school reunion, I met old friends who I could feel had, in their view, fallen short of their youthful dreams. It was painful to listen to their stories, excuses and rationalizations.

DISCOVERING NEW PATHS

Each generation cries out from its own moment, searching for meaning within its age and cultural assumptions. Today people are embarking on a bewildering assortment of quests for spiritual enlightenment, a need which has emerged from and is given impetus by a century dominated by rationalism.

I'm a war baby, born in 1942. The 1950s was my school era, and the turbulent 1960s my university period. Each generation finds a focus, both out of necessity and interest. Landon Jones reflects that in the 1960s we studied sociology to change our world; in the 1970s, psychology to change ourselves; in the 1980s, business management to guarantee our economic future; and in the 1990s we studied the environment to insure we have a place in which to live.

Attention is being directed to issues about spirituality, an interest that flies in the face of the dominating scientific materialism, which defined the twentieth century. Two factors have fueled this fascination with the spiritual and rejection of the rational as being the only way to learn truth. First is the metaphysical hype that accompanies shifting from one century to the next. The turn of the nineteenth to twentieth centuries was marked by a rise in new forms of Western-flavored religion, including Christian Science, founded by Mary Baker Eddy. Then, as we approached the twenty-first century, there were expectations that either we would face a collapse of world systems or unbounded freedom and peace would dawn. The buildup to the third millennium flowed from the radical days of the 1960s, which included a growing interest in spirituality. During the last few decades of the twentieth century, increased forms of spiritual manifestation kept popping up, involving everything from modern-day Asian mystics to baby-boom churches in North America, such as the 15,000-member Willowcreek Community Church on the outskirts of Chicago.

Bernice Boyes and I first met at a writers' conference at Briercrest College in southern Saskatchewan. Because of a condition with which she was born (myositis ossificans progressiva, a disease in which the fluid in a bruise turns into hardened calcium), by the time she was in her early twenties, walking was difficult, her arms became increasingly immobile, and eventually she could move about only in a wheelchair. I was amazed at her resilience and optimism. One day I opened a parcel, and there was a painting she had done for Lily and me. What an exercise of love!

Though Bernice was honest about her condition, it didn't keep her from talking about her dreams. One day after receiving our family picture, she said, "Brian, even though I am trapped in this body, which is anything but attractive, and even though I know I will never marry and have a family, I have the same desire for intimacy, loving and parenting as others do." My heart ached for her. What counsel could I offer? I would be untruthful if I pretended her hopes would be realized. I knew she wouldn't marry, and I realized her life expectancy was short. However, locked in her deteriorating body, she refused to be bound. One day she wrote:

> I am not disabled. If you were to look at a picture of me in my wheelchair, you might want to question that, but let me explain. Most of us want to be accepted primarily for who we are and what we can contribute to society. How short we are, how tall, how thin, how stout, how beautiful, how plain—we don't want to be judged by such factors. We can be four foot eight inches, scrawny, with a big nose and two left feet but have a "heart" the size of Texas.

So then, if we look beyond appearance, I am not disabled. My body happens to be, but I am not. Does this change how we view a person with a disability when we meet them? I think it should.

Over the years, I've seen a variety of reactions to my disability, ranging from the bizarre to the disappointing. There was the boy who thought I was someone's science project when he saw my friend pushing me in my wheelchair one day. Then there were those who told me not to bother completing high school because it would be too difficult for me to handle the workload.

Since then I have started a career in writing, been on a Christian mission trip and participated in disability research and government negotiations. I don't plan to spend my time merely filling my days playing bingo or watching talk shows as some might expect me to. Life has all kinds of potential!

My disability is not the worst thing that could ever happen to me. I know people who have no physical needs to speak of, but are severely "handicapped" because of the troubles they've experienced in life and how they've chosen to handle them. We all have challenges, strengths and weaknesses. I can help you with yours, and you can help me with mine.

You see, when it gets right down to it, everyone has a disablement of some kind, be it physical, emotional or spiritual. I believe that handicaps of the soul are infinitely more intense than any physical disability. And healing of our souls through the forgiving love of Jesus is infinitely more critical than physical healing (although that can happen, too).

Bernice hurt both physically and emotionally. But that didn't deter her from living a life filled with adventure, public concern and prayer.

There is a way out of suffering. It doesn't deny pain's existence; neither does it find its solution in "ten easy steps." The way out is tough and demanding, requiring effort and time. As surely as pain is real, so is healing. It's not lifted from a pop-culture fix-it bag of tricks. Neither is it a language of New Age psycho-babble. It does not deny modern medicine's ability to correct chemical imbalances; neither does it ignore our increased understanding of mind/body relationships nor the enormous strides in the ability of care providers to assist us by way of therapy. Indeed it celebrates what we have learned and what we can do now.

This path to healing is three-fold, taking us on a journey through hope, faith and love. It is much older than modern therapy. Many have walked this ancient passage. Its essentials have been tested by wise sages, by those who have struggled for survival in the deepest places of despair. And it has been walked by the very giver of life itself. The path is not a simple self-help formula. If that is all it is, then we would be alone in our pain, having to help ourselves walk the path. Though it involves all of who we are (and in that sense, we must work at helping ourselves), if all we can do is help ourselves, then despair is the fitting response: "I have no one else to help me." Unique to this path is the promise that we are not alone.

The journey to healing helps us see who we are and to understand our connection to the rest of creation. It helps us tap into the eternal wisdom of the ages so that our inner selves are nourished, our minds released of despair, our broken hearts mended and our human natures released so we can live as we were intended.

Since childhood I've been fascinated by my father's Swedish ancestry. In the summertime our family would often drive eastward some 800 kilometers from Saskatoon to the farms of our Swedish relatives near Minnedosa, in southwestern Manitoba. I'd listen to the gentle, rolling Swedish vowels as Dad would exchange childhood stories with aunts Edith and Elsie and uncles Alan, Henning and Ted. With that memory of family, I've searched for a link to our European roots. Now that my father and his brother are dead, with no written history and few records, my search had little to go on. It began in earnest in 1990, when a friend and I traveled to Sweden to research the history of my dad's mother. What I learned was not what I had imagined our past to be.

We went north of Stockholm to the Baltic port of Umeå and then west to Vänessä to meet a distant relative of mine, John Norberg, who explained the family tree. On a Sunday morning, he began unraveling the story of Grandma Hanna Stiller, and I began to learn of her past and to piece together the events and places of her early life. He'd tell me about her only as we drove from site to site, places important to her story. It was like sitting in live theater, waiting while the scenery changed behind closed curtains.

The pilgrimage began at the homestead of Per Persson, grandfather to Grandma Stiller. The farm house was just as I imagined, a large well-constructed building alongside a wide, flowing river, elegant and well preserved, obviously the home of a prosperous family. What a pleasant way to begin a look into my past.

We left that home, and after driving some miles, John parked the car by Lake Ostansjo, walked up a hill, stopped at a clearing and said, "Here is where your great-grandfather Jon Hansson and your great-grandmother Maria Margareta set up their first home, and here is where their six children were born, including your grandmother."

"What an idyllic spot," I said.

John paused, seemingly reluctant to go on. He looked away, speaking slowly and softly, "Something happened to Jon Hansson, your great-grandfather. He was sent to a mental institution over in Umeå. To protect her children, your great-grandmother Maria Margareta got a divorce around 1880."

The picturesque landscape lost its charm. I felt robbed, as if the facts of the past had no right to intrude on my imagination. The surrounding scenery took on a new look. The tree in the center of the clearing seemed different. As I looked down on Lake Ostansjo, I imagined the heartache and sense of desperation as Maria Margareta sought to care for and protect her six children. I wanted to forget it all and leave with my idealized vision intact, but I was compelled to follow the trail. We got back in the car. I was lost in my thoughts and John respectfully gave me time to absorb this disturbing history.

Next we pulled into a farmyard. John said, "Here your great-

grandmother raised her six children. After Jon Hansson was sent away, Maria asked one of her brothers to build her a house. So he built a one-room log house. It was here, alone, that Maria, a peasant living during one of the worst famines in Swedish history, raised your grandmother and her brothers and sisters."

I walked up to the door; the owner stepped back to let me in. The old log house had been stripped to its original logs and fireplace. I looked around—just one room—where great-grandmother Maria raised her family. I stood still and closed my eyes, imagining the cries of hunger, aloneness and anxiety. Over 100 years ago, Maria raised my Grandma Stiller and her five siblings without a father, no social security and in grinding poverty.

I left the homestead reluctantly. On one hand I wanted to pretend this had never happened, and yet I wanted to feel the hurt and heartache of the great-grandmother I never knew. We climbed back in the car and drove down the country road to the next place of harsh memories. We turned into a farm and drove around the house to the backyard. John said, "See that small cabin? That's where Jon Hansson, your great-grandfather, lived out his life after years in the mental hospital."

I walked into the small log cabin behind the main house where his sister had lived. I ran my hands over the carpentry bench where he had made furniture, trying to imagine him as he sorted out his feelings and heartache. (Later I learned that those who worshipped in the "free" church and celebrated communion apart from the state church were treated harshly. Often the father of the family would be sent to either prison or an insane asylum.) For whatever reason Hansson was sent away, our past is a tragic story of a young family who started the journey of life in brokenness.

Crossing back across the Atlantic, I thought of Grandma Stiller, struck first by her parents' divorce—unimaginable in that day— raised in a single room in days of famine. Grandma Stiller later married and had a son, but both her husband and son died. She then left Sweden and sailed for Canada, took the train to the Canadian prairie city of Winnipeg, and in the Swedish Covenant Church on Logan Avenue, met August Stiller who had emigrated from Sweden more than a decade earlier. From that marriage came two sons, my father Carl Hilmer Stiller and his brother August Henning Stiller, and their forty-nine children, grandchildren and great-grandchildren.

As I write, our son Murray calls from Vancouver and tells us the good news that his wife Catherine has given birth to their first child (our first grandchild), Pearson Carl David Stiller. Hearing of the birth of one's first grandchild is a special moment. After the phone call I wonder, If I could ask Grandma Stiller for her wish for her great-great-grandson, would she want his life spared of the hardships and sorrows she experienced? I'm sure she would. What I do know is that, even with the setbacks and hardships of her childhood and adult life, Hanna Stiller set in motion a family now strong in faith, surrounded with nurturing sibling love and tradition. Through her hope, faith and love, our entire family is now rich beyond what she could have imagined. We are inheritors of her life.

Les Tarr was, in my view, possibly the most outstanding Christian journalist in Canada in the last half of the twentieth century. He began after serving as church minister in Winnipeg, where he contracted tubercular meningitis. No longer able to serve in that position, he turned to writing. Eventually he ended up bedridden, plagued by phantom pain. He hurt so much that morphine was the only way to circumvent the debilitating pain.

From his bed, scratching with a writing apparatus strapped to his arm, Les spoke. He was tough on the Christian community when it deserved it and unrelenting on the arrogance of the secular media when they made no attempt to understand the nature of faith.

I watched as he and his wife Catherine continued to read, research, publish and boldly write, even as pain wracked his body. The pain and sheer inconvenience could have ended his sense of vision and purpose. It could have discontinued his enormous output of critical thinking. But it didn't. Even with the plaguing hurt, his life continued, defined and nurtured by his understanding of God's purpose.

Many who walk the path of suffering find a way to healing, usually different from what they had expected. My brother Dave and Evelyn didn't get their Jill back. Bernice was never freed from being trapped in a deteriorating body. Grandma Stiller was not able to undo her childhood, and Les Tarr didn't find a day without pain. Yet they all found hope and rose to new ways of living, all the while discovering the enormous power there is in a life beyond themselves.

As you progress along this path of healing, don't view this book as a manual on pain. Neither should it replace the important work of a therapist. It is not a substitute for professional care. For those in trauma who are beyond their ability to cope, the role of a professional caregiver in providing balanced and insightful emotional and psychological help is essential. We have been given the gifts of help by therapists and medical science, and when properly used these will provide insights and possibly lead to a prescribed means of healing. This book is written as a supplement, to encourage you on your personal journey, helping you to see how faith can bring healing and life to you day by day.

The three-fold path of hope, faith and love is progressive. It begins where you are. It recognizes that in the trauma of hurt, the progression out of suffering takes time. The beginning point is to see that life is not only what you feel now. In learning to walk this path out from the malaise of sadness, we are called on to make conscious choices so that feelings are called into line with what we decide is best.

To continue in emotional pain is not the intention of creation. There is a path of healing.

Two

OPEN A NEW WINDOW OF HOPE

When trapped in a downward swirl of personal tragedy and sorrow, to see anything else but our own hurt is difficult. We get caught in trying to manage powerful emotions, while at the same time, trying to sort out overriding problems. At that moment perspective means everything.

If you have lost a loved one, for example, people will try to say in the nicest of ways, "Well, things will look different a year from now."

"Why, of course things will," we want to shout. "That's not the issue. It's how I feel *now* that matters."

However, looking down the road of time is important. That's called perspective. Consider the metaphor of a window, built through interaction with family, friends, school and community, all contributing to the way we learn to see and interpret life. A child nurtured in a loving and secure home will learn to see through a different window than one raised in a stress-filled home of distrust and violence. In adulthood we continue to see life from the perspective we developed as we grew. The challenge is not to let the window keep us trapped, so we are unable to see outside its confining borders. We must open it to see all the possibilities before us.

I have heard many times, "Tell us how we can find hope and release in this moment of sorrow."

The point is not to remake the tragedy, making it appear as if it had some redeeming value. Neither can one undo the past. What has been done is done. If I had wasted my young adult life stoned on drugs, I couldn't go back and redeem those years. They would be lost, and lost forever. The way is not back but forward. Our journey is not back to the garden of innocence but forward to the City of God (as conceived by Augustine).

We can, though, out of past tragedies learn that life need not be determined by tragedy. The Nazi Holocaust of the 1930s and 1940s is an example. One cannot visit the relics of Auschwitz or come away from the Holocaust memorial of Yad Vashem in Israel without being deeply touched.

However, the world now has a community that has lit the enduring flame of "never again," a light that illumines the dark face of racism, wherever it may be. We can't return to the Treaty of Versailles and expunge the fear and anger of the German people. Neither can we erase fascism's dehumanizing notion of a superior race. Those factors were years in the making. But we can face similar realities in other places and name them for what they are. Whether we look through a window defined by our experience or open it wide to expand our possibilities determines how we will respond to events and circumstances, be they personal or societal.

A WINDOW OF HOPE

The point of departure on the path to healing is hope. Hope helps us see outside our hurt, past the plaguing fear, gripping dread, unnerving anxiety and paralyzing despair. It isn't a simplistic, "I'll pick myself up by the bootstraps," but it is a realization that all of life is not as we currently see it. To hope is to see what our pain and hurt won't allow us to see. And to see through that window calls for effort. Hope doesn't fall from the sky.

Hope, the first stage on the road to healing, leads to faith. Hope is seeing life as what it could be, not as what it is.

Elisha, a Jewish prophet, stirred up the anger of an opposing army that was trying to overrun Israel. The invading king, thinking Elisha had given the king of Israel information on their whereabouts, surrounded the prophet's home during the night. In the morning Elisha's servant, frightened when he saw their town surrounded by the enemy army, asked, "What can we do?"

Elisha's prayer was simply this: "Lord, open his eyes so he can see." His servant turned and, to his surprise, saw beyond the enemy army surrounding the village to the army of the Lord. Instead of seeing only "what was," the servant, seeing through a window of hope, saw "what else."

Charles Swindoll puts it this way:

> When trapped in a tunnel of misery, hope points to the light at the end.
> When we are overworked and exhausted, hope gives us fresh energy.
> When we are discouraged, hope lifts our spirits.
> When we are tempted to quit, hope keeps us going.
> When we've lost our way and confusion blurs the destination, hope dulls the edge of panic.
> When we struggle with a crippling disease or a lingering illness, hope helps us persevere beyond pain.
> When we fear the worst, hope brings reminders that God is still in control.
> When we must endure the consequences of bad decisions, hope refuels our recovery.
> When we find ourselves unemployed, hope tells us we still have a future.
> When we are forced to sit back, hope gives us the patience to trust.
> When we feel rejected and abandoned, hope reminds us we're not alone . . . we'll make it.
> When we say our final farewell to someone we love, hope in the life beyond get us through our grief.[1]

A character from the New Testament offers another illustration of hope:

As Jesus entered the village of Capernaum, a Roman captain came up

21

in a panic and said, "Master, my servant is sick. He can't walk. He's in terrible pain."

Jesus said, "I'll come and heal him."

"Oh, no," said the captain. "I don't want to put you to all that trouble. Just give the order and my servant will be fine. I'm a man who takes orders and gives orders. I tell one soldier, 'Go,' and he goes; to another, 'Come,' and he comes; to my slave, 'Do this,' and he does it."

Taken aback, Jesus said, "I've yet to come across this kind of simple trust in Israel, the very people who are supposed to know all about God and how he works. This man is the vanguard of many outsiders who will soon be coming from all directions—streaming in from the east, pouring in from the west, sitting down at God's kingdom banquet alongside Abraham, Isaac and Jacob. Then those who grew up 'in the faith' but had no faith will find themselves out in the cold, outsiders to grace and wondering what happened."

Then Jesus turned to the captain and said, "Go. What you believed could happen has happened." At that moment his servant became well (Matt. 8:5–13).

There are two forces at work here. The first is the hope the captain has in the ability of Jesus. He knows Jesus can heal his servant. The second is that of faith: Jesus not only can make the man well, but he will.

Hope is a way of seeing "what else." To put it another way, hope is the frame that is provided for the picture. The Roman captain was far from being included in the healing agenda of this Jewish rabbi. At the time, Rome was the invader, oppressing Jewish citizens who hated the Romans. But even more, this man was more than a soldier, he was a Roman captain. It was preposterous for him to imagine that Jesus would listen to him. Yet, in the face of that, the captain came to Jesus. Undoubtedly he had heard Jesus' teachings and watched him heal. We don't know if the captain was optimistic, but we do know he overcame this formidable social distance and presented his case to Jesus. His action shows how determined he was: by opening a window of hope, he included himself in Jesus' agenda.

STEPS ON THE PATH

We use the word *hope* in many ways: "I hope to see you"; "Where there is life there is hope"; "Hope doesn't disappoint us"; "All we can do is pray and hope"; "I hope you have a really good time"; or as Alexander Pope said, "Hope springs eternal."

Such usage is helpful, but when you are in a vice-like grip of sorrow, you want to know which path to take. The path of hope is identified by five signposts: belief, trust, possibilities, determination and realism.

BELIEF

Often we confuse belief as being the same as faith. Here is the difference: even though we may believe something to be true, it doesn't mean we have faith in it for ourselves. For example, you may believe that a rope bridge strung across a valley is strong enough to hold you, but not have faith to trust your life on it.

However, belief is essential to the positioning of oneself in hope. The captain believed that Jesus was able to care for his need. We don't know if he had faith to the extent that he became a disciple and gave up his career or the worship of Caesar. But he did believe in this rabbi to the extent that he was prepared to make the approach. In the end he came to Jesus, believing he had the power to heal his servant.

TRUST

This is the step beyond belief. By trusting we put ourselves into the hands of a person or community. Note that the captain trusted to the point that he made his request in a crowd; he didn't catch Jesus at a time or a place where others wouldn't see or hear him with this rabbi who worried Roman authorities. He caught up to Jesus in the public square of Capernaum, in northern Galilee.

POSSIBILITIES

The captain had various possibilities: his Roman doctors and the local medical practitioners. Yet he chose to approach Jesus. Could it have been that he had tried others, and they had failed his servant?

Is hope another word for optimism? In a sense it is. It frames one's mind with the possibility of healing. However, the problem with the language of optimism is that it is overly associated with emotional hype and simplistic formulas. Promoters and conferences can load their lectures with emotional stories, but after peer enthusiasm is over, there is no emotional or cognitive foundation on which ongoing health can be constructed. Optimism as an emotion is very important. Hope, however, goes further. It frames what we believe.

DETERMINATION

Hope doesn't come easily. It takes more than mantra chants or chest beating to find hope. It requires a willingness to open the window through which we see the future. This is tough. We need more than platitudes such as, "When the going gets tough, the tough get going." To come into hope requires determination to begin a new way of thinking.

Even though Les Tarr was overshadowed by excruciating phantom pain, he was determined to frame his life so his gifts would continue to produce brilliant insights and allow him to craft his journalistic pieces.

REALISM

Hope framed in fantasy and foolishness breeds heartache and disappointment. This is where people go wrong. Caught in the trauma of intense hurt, be it physical pain, emotional abuse or the loneliness of bereavement, one is vulnerable to charlatans or well-meaning people whose ideas can be foolish, shallow and impractical. Hope, no matter how sincere, is vulnerable to abuse when based on unrealistic ideas, unwise people or self-serving systems. But when rooted in a larger reality, it withstands surrounding foolishness. Here's an illustration:

As my wife Lily and I approached the main entrance to the Basilica and Shrine of Our Lady of Fatima in central Portugal, I was offended by the crass commercialism of the shops lining the streets leading up to this world-famous destination of pilgrims. Hawkers of all sorts sold their garish figurines, all promising various miracles. We walked into the basilica and followed the line past the coffin of the Carmelite nun Lucia Santos. As we did, I saw an old woman standing in line to say her confession. Her face was like none I had ever seen. Dressed in typical peasant garb, a black dress with a black head scarf, she stood alone awaiting her turn. Her face, lined with years of hard work, told a story of a hard life. Yet there was a sense of hope calling her to this place of faith. As tacky as the surrounding paraphernalia was, it could not overshadow her belief that she could count on the realism of a Christian faith rooted in history and truth, promising God's love and eternal forgiveness.

I am chagrined by miracle-promising hustlers who perform their religious acts. While I cringe at their antics and am annoyed by their self-promoting excesses, when all of the blustery tub-thumping is over and the religious props have been packed away for another show, Jesus Christ continues to stand at the center of history with his promise of healing, as he did for this peasant woman at the basilica.

FREEDOM IN HOPE

Fear holds you in prison; hope sets your spirit free. Few writers have caught this theme with greater clarity than has Viktor Frankl, the Swiss psychiatrist and practitioner of hope who survived the Nazi death camps. Out of his near-death imprisonment, Frankl looked into the human spirit and discovered the meaning and nature of hope. Developing his theory of logotherapy he wrote, "The prisoner who has lost faith in the future, 'his future,' was doomed. With his loss of belief in the future, he also lost his spiritual hold; he let himself decline and became subject to mental and physical decay. Usually this happened quite suddenly, in the form of crisis, the symptoms of which were familiar to the experienced camp inmate."[2]

His frank explanation of why some prisoners survived and others didn't is important. Frankl understood that at the heart of human survival is hope. We can be overcome by debilitating memories which can cause all manner of dysfunction. Much of modern psychotherapy is devoted to discovering past violations and hurts and bringing wounds to the open so that salve can be applied for proper and long-lasting healing. What Frankl showed us is that, although the present is shaped by our past, what helps us recreate the present is our vision and hope of the future. He saw inmates struggling to survive, some driven deep into despair. One of his close friends gave up and died of disappointment just days before they were liberated by the Allies. Others were lifted by their deep belief and hope in something beyond the present. In other words, they were transformed by their vision of the future. Frankl wrote, "Whoever was still alive had reason to hope. Health, family, happiness, professional abilities, fortune, position in society—all these were things that could be achieved again or restored. . . . I asked the poor creatures who listened to me attentively in the darkness of the hut to face up to the seriousness of our position. They must not lose hope but should keep courage in the certainty that the hopelessness of our struggle did not detract from its dignity and its meaning."[3]

While fear holds you in prison, hope gives you freedom to open the windows made by your spirit.

Lily Rogers and I met in our first year of college in 1960. The next summer I hitchhiked some 1,200 kilometers from my home in

Saskatoon, Saskatchewan, to her place in Kenora, Ontario, located on the famous Lake of the Woods. I was attracted to this young music teacher and was hopeful our relationship would grow. I arrived one summer afternoon and was invited to her home for dinner. In the course of the conversation, I learned more about her family's past.

Olive and Frank Rogers had married in 1936; they had one son and two daughters. When Lily, their eldest girl, was fifteen, Frank took sick with cancer and died. Their son Albert was seventeen and their younger daughter Elsie, eleven. Olive, now left with three, had no job and no training in work outside the home, and little insurance. Thankfully, the house Frank had built on Mellick Avenue was paid for.

So what is a forty-three-year-old single mother to do? The only available job she could find was cleaning offices at the lumber mill. So for twenty years, five days a week, she would leave her family at 4:00 p.m., walk down the hill and work until midnight.

As I got to know Olive Rogers, I saw a person who, in her struggle to keep a home and raise three teenagers, did so with profound hope and trust. There were few I had met who matched the deep and sustaining hope that pervaded her life. In the long hours of hard work, she continued to love and pray for her own children and for those in the Sunday school class she taught in the little church just up the street.

During these long, hard years, she not only had hope for her children, but she dreamed that some day she would be an artist. Eventually, hands worn by the harshness of cleaning became the gifted and sensitive hands that painted canvases and sculpted figurines. Her paintings won awards, and today they grace many a home. My favorite of her paintings hangs in our dining room: a winter scene with a cottage set against snowy hills.

Olive's life was shaped by hope. Amid the seeming hopelessness of Frank's death, she saw through the window of God's provision. In her loneliness as a young widow, did she ever believe God would let her down? Did she ever wonder, during the back-breaking tasks at the mill office, whether this window of hope was foolish? The evenings were long and difficult, but she had a vision of what might be, and by faith and determination she painted a picture for our family. There have been few who brought such rich textures of hope and determination to our children and grandchildren as this beautiful, life-giving mother of God's creation, Olive Rogers.

❖

Towards the latter part of Jesus' life, he told the disciples of his approaching death to be followed by his coming back to life, something they couldn't grasp. Here is part of that conversation, which was held during his last meal. His description of his coming death

> stirred up a hornet's nest of questions among the disciples: "What's he talking about: 'In a day or so you're not going to see me, but then in another day or so you will see me'? And, 'Because I'm on my way to the Father'? What is this 'day or so'? We don't know what he is talking about."
>
> Jesus knew they were dying to ask him what he meant, so he said, "Are you trying to figure out among yourselves what I meant when I said, 'In a day or so you're not going to see me, but then in another day or so you will see me'? Then fix this firmly in your minds: You're going to be in deep mourning while the godless world throws a party. You'll be sad, very sad, but your sadness will develop into gladness.
>
> "When a woman gives birth, she has a hard time, there's no getting around it. But when the baby is born, there is joy in the birth. This new life in the world wipes out memory of the pain. The sadness you have right now is similar to that pain, but the coming joy is also similar. When I see you again, you'll be full of joy, and it will be a joy no one can rob from you. . . .
>
> "This is what I want you to do: Ask the Father for whatever is in keeping with the things I've revealed to you. Ask in my name, according to my will, and he'll most certainly give it to you. Your joy will be a river overflowing its banks!" (John 16:16–24)

Jesus knew the disciples would be caught in fear and would forget his words. Even so, he tried to build in their minds a new way of seeing, so when he arose from the dead, they would look at events through an open window.

The point is that, as we walk this path of hope, regardless of the devastating event and no matter how bleak the future, the promise is ours that his joy will be ours, if we choose to take that path.

HOPE MEANS A RECOGNITION THAT HURT IS NOT THE END OF LIFE

Hurt is neither the end of our life on Earth, nor is it the end of life altogether. We usually consider life in the here and now. When tragedy strikes, we often say, "My life is over," in the sense that there is no more meaning or purpose. It's here that hope calls us away from despair, which tells us there is nothing more. Hope doesn't give in. While we may feel we don't want to go on, the flickering candle of hope refuses to let darkness take over.

The Old Testament prophet, in foretelling the Messiah, offers this description:

> A bruised reed he will not break,
> and a smoldering wick he will not snuff out (Isa. 42:3).

In life's struggles, the Creator sees our hurt in such a way as to help us move past our point of failure. The bruised or weakened reed will not be broken in two. The reed is not berated for its bruise. Instead his coming enables the reed to rebuild and grow, finding new life.

Charles Colson, an aide to former President Nixon, who was convicted and jailed for his Watergate crimes, began Prison Fellowship, a ministry for convicts in prison. The organization chose a broken reed for its symbol, a perfect metaphor for loving and helping people caught by their failings, trapped by webs of guilt and self recrimination. The work of the Messiah opens windows on the hurting soul. Through these windows we see opportunities of faith and love as we make the journey.

HOPE IS THE BELIEF THAT PHYSICAL DEATH IS NOT THE END

As we stand by the casket of a loved one, watching as it is lowered into the waiting grave, and hear the familiar words, "Dust to dust, and ashes to ashes," we know that this too is not the end. Peter Kreeft says that if there is no life after death, then suffering is a death pang and not a birth pang. The pang of hurt in suffering can mean only birth or death. It can open the way to new thinking, feeling, living and serving, or it can be the end. It really becomes our choice. But there is no more central theme or reality in Christian faith than that of hope. Life is never at an end.

HOPE BEGINS THE PROCESS OF OPENING WINDOWS

During my earlier years of public ministry, in my desire to build our personal finances, I got involved in an investment requiring personal guarantees. Without my knowledge, one of my partners took proceeds from our investment and sunk it in a scheme that went bankrupt. The banks then came looking for us to make good on our guarantees, which meant losing our home. I felt my public ministry was over. I assumed that I'd be so discredited that whatever I did would be undermined. It was a dark moment.

I learned a lesson in a strange way. One evening at our family cottage, I was sitting alone down by the lake, contemplating the coming financial disaster. We had no more resources, and I concluded all we could do was to declare personal bankruptcy. The sun had set, and floodlights from the cottage played their shadows around me. A noise to my right drew my attention. I turned and saw a large forbidding shadow moving towards me. Earlier that summer we had discovered a bear den at the back of our property, and so in my mind

I saw the shadow as being that of a bear. Not being a hero when it comes to bears, I froze. I didn't know whether to call out for help from Lily, jump in the lake or run. In my fright I took another look, and there was our lovable sheltie dog Heidi. Only as I looked more carefully did I realize that shadows had made her appear larger than life. I had confused the shadows with reality.

I resolved to re-examine our financial situation. In the end our home was saved and the bank issue resolved. But it took my adopting a different way of seeing.

HOPE IS A BELIEF THAT SUFFERING IS NOT IN VAIN

Hurt and suffering have a way of preventing us from seeing the deeper meaning of life. In the first days of personal tragedy, numbness holds us back from making progress. We must not rush past the important moments of grieving. Hope does not discount the importance and necessity of allowing a period of grief. But once some time has allowed the intensity of the hurt to subside, hope calls us to believe beyond our feelings and begin to see that—illogical as it may seem—meaning can be found in tragedy.

Turning again to the insights of the Swiss psychiatrist Viktor Frankl,

> If there is meaning in life at all, then there must be a meaning in suffering. Suffering is an ineradicable part of life. I was struggling to find the reason for my sufferings, my slow dying. In a last violent protest against the hopelessness of imminent death, I sensed my spirit piercing through the enveloping gloom. I felt it transcend that helpless, meaningless world, and from somewhere I heard a victorious "Yes" in answer to my question of the existence of an ultimate purpose.
>
> Man's main concern is not to gain pleasure or to avoid pain, but rather to see a meaning in his life. That is why man is even ready to suffer, on the condition, to be sure, that his suffering has a meaning.[4]

In the filth, violence and heartbreak of the Nazi camps, Frankl learned that suffering was not meaningless.

HOPE GIVES US THE KNOWLEDGE THAT OUR LIVES CAN BE ENRICHED, REGARDLESS OF THE SEVERITY OF OUR HURT

If we believe that our lives can grow even in the desert, hope calls us to the next stage of seeing that suffering is not in vain.

Malcolm Muggeridge, the twentieth-century English writer and broadcaster put it this way:

> Contrary to what might be expected, I look back on experiences that at the time seemed especially desolating and painful with particular satisfaction. Indeed, I can say with complete truthfulness that everything I have learned in my seventy-five years in this world, everything that has truly enhanced and enlightened my existence, has been through affliction and not through happiness. In other words, if it ever were to be possible to eliminate affliction from our earthly existence by means of some drug or other medical mumbo jumbo . . . the result would not be to make life delectable, but to make it too banal and trivial to be endurable. This, of course, is what the Cross signifies. And it is the Cross, more than anything else, that has called me inexorably to Christ.[5]

In biblical times, Joseph, the son of a wealthy landowner, was kidnapped by his brothers and sold to slave traders who in turn sold him as a slave in Egypt. Often his life was endangered. One such experience was caused by the wife of an army general who tried to seduce Joseph while her husband was at the battlefront. Frightened by the possible consequences, Joseph ran from her rooms. In her anger, she accused him of rape, and he was subsequently thrown into jail. While in jail Joseph assisted some inmates, who, grateful for Joseph's help, promised that upon their release, they would put in a good word for him. But although they were released they never tried to help him, and Joseph remained in prison.

In spite of injustice and forgotten promises, Joseph eventually rose to become prime minister of Egypt. One day, in response to a query from the Pharaoh about a dream, Joseph warned of seven years of good crops to be followed by seven years of famine. The Pharaoh gave Joseph the job of stockpiling supplies for the disaster he predicted would come. Back home in Israel, Joseph's family also experienced the drought. In an effort to survive, his father sent Joseph's brothers to Egypt to buy grain, not knowing that their brother was running a massive food enterprise.

When they arrived, Joseph recognized his brothers but didn't reveal his identity. After playing some sly games, he finally realized that even though his brothers had hated him and sold him to slave traders, "you intended to harm me, but God intended it for good" (Gen. 50:20).

He learned that even in the years of personal anguish and humiliation, there was another way of seeing his own tragedy. By walking the path of hope, he was called on to rescue the very ones who had done him wrong.

In one car accident, Gerald Sittser lost his wife, daughter and mother. He wrote, "Pain is a gift because it shows we have a capacity to feel, whether pain in the body or pain in the soul. . . . Pain therefore is the flip side of pleasure. The nerves that tell us of one also tell us of the other. . . . Ears that cringe at the wail of a siren also listen with pleasure to a Beethoven symphony."[6]

By assuming that pain is always bad, we go to enormous lengths to cover it up. All the while the pain we attempt to quiet is speaking to us about an underlying reality, and the symptoms cry out for proper diagnostic remedy.

The path of hope brings healing, life and new realities. In a very real sense, we help to create a new future when we begin our journey. Without taking those first steps we will never know what is ahead. The path of hope is the prelude to the challenging path of faith. As we walk this first leg of the journey, we link up with opportunities we can't foresee.

Three

THE RISK-TAKING PATH
OF FAITH

In the late 1800s the Great Blondin, a high-wire artist, advertised he would cross the Niagara Falls gorge on a guy wire. The crowds arrived early, and when the showman stepped up and asked, "How many believe I can cross over and return?" there was a burst of applause. Without a further word, he inched his way across the river and back to the thrill of the onlookers.

He then pointed to a wheelbarrow and asked, "How many believe I can push this wheelbarrow across and return?" A deafening applause was the answer.

After his return Blondin called out to the crowd, "How many believe I can push this wheelbarrow across with someone in it?" There were no doubters in the crowd. They voiced their belief by hooting and clapping.

Then he asked, "Who will be the first volunteer?" He was greeted with stony silence.

All the spectators believed he could and would do as he promised. They even believed he could traverse the gorge with someone in the wheelbarrow. But no one had faith to risk his or her life.

We often confuse the words *hope, belief* and *faith*, as if they mean the same. Hope is seeing possibilities, as in "I have hope for the future." Belief is the assumption that what I hope in is true. Faith is acting on what I believe by taking the next step of risk.

The Hebrew story of the people of Israel crossing into the Promised Land helps us see the difference between hope and faith. Moses had led them out of Egypt in the Exodus, but because they lacked faith in the promises of Yahweh (the Hebrew word for Lord), they ended up wandering some forty years in the wilderness.

Moses eventually died, and the young general Joshua took over. His role as leader was soon tested as he guided hundreds of thousands through the Palestinian wilderness. As his followers inched their way up the east side of the Jordan River, they could see across to the land earlier promised to their father Abraham. Standing on the east side, Joshua knew the restless Israelites were watching him, wondering what he would do.

He called out, "Consecrate yourselves, for tomorrow the Lord will do amazing things among you" (Josh. 3:5). Joshua operated with hope, conveying his belief that God would lead them. Faith had yet to be exercised, but he had set the stage for himself and his people.

The next day the word came from Yahweh: "Tell the priests who carry the ark of the covenant: 'When you reach the edge of the Jordan's waters, go and stand in the river'" (Josh. 3:8). Now Joshua had his direction. But would he be willing to subject himself to the scrutiny of those he was leading? This was his test of faith.

Joshua not only had hope and belief, he had faith. Acting in faith he commanded, "As soon as the priests who carry the ark of the Lord set foot in the Jordan, its waters flowing downstream will be cut off and stand up in a heap" (Josh. 3:13).

He believed in God and had faith that God would do as promised. While Joshua led in the spirit of hope, that wasn't enough. He had to take the next risky step and direct the priests to move out into the water. That was faith: acting on his belief and, by so doing, bringing the promise into reality. That's the difference between hope and faith. Faith doesn't operate without hope, for it is hope that creates the environment of what is possible. But hope is nothing more than optimism if it doesn't clinch reality into place by faith. One path leads to the next: hope to belief to faith.

"As soon as the priests who carried the ark reached the Jordan and their feet touched the water's edge, the water from upstream stopped flowing" (Josh. 3:15–16), and they walked across the Jordan River on dry ground.

WHAT FAITH IS NOT

Faith is often trumped up to mean many things. To help us more clearly link faith to how we live, we must note what faith is not.

A BLIND LEAP

Some compare faith to a blind leap, using the metaphor of a child leaping into darkness at the call of a parent. Such understanding of faith is opposite to biblical faith. To trust Christ is to act by faith in a person we know and not someone in the dark. Our eyes are wide open; we see who he is. This Jesus was right out in public: his life was foretold, and his arrival was public. He defined his kingdom in the public places of Palestine. His life is recorded in public documents, and for two thousand years, we have come to know his life and mission. It is anything but a blind leap.

MASS HYSTERIA

Those who resort to mind control in administering their message of healing capitalize on emotional hysteria. Understandably, people are most vulnerable to promises when their physical and emotional wellbeing is at stake. In a sense, they'll try anything. Thus a dynamic, emotional speaker can manipulate people into believing most anything. But faith is not synonymous with hysteria. Instead, biblical faith is rooted in an understanding that life is linked to a loving and healing Creator. If one believes that emotional manipulation is the result of God at work, a person will be left disappointed, cynical and hurt.

RELIGION

We often refer to a person as being "of faith," meaning he believes in or is a member of a particular religion. Though this is convenient verbal shorthand, there is an important difference between being part of a particular faith and living by faith. To have faith in Christ means one has chosen to walk in the ways of Jesus Christ. Faith begins with a belief that the Scriptures are trustworthy, which in turn provides the means whereby we can come to know Jesus. As we come to believe in Jesus Christ, we progress to committing our lives to him.

SO, WHAT IS FAITH?

We have seen that faith, operating through hope and belief, connects us with what is possible. Then as we respond to God's promises, his life becomes ours.

A Jewish writer puts it this way: "Now faith is being sure of what we hope for and certain of what we do not see" (Heb. 11:1, NIV). In *The Message*, Eugene Peterson sees the text this way: "The fundamental fact of existence is that this trust in God, this faith, is the firm foundation under everything that makes life worth living. It's our handle on what we can't see. The act of faith is what distinguished our ancestors, set them above the crowd." The King James version of the Bible says, "Now faith is the substance of things hoped for, the evidence of things not seen."

Simply put, faith is acting based on what we believe is true. But faith doesn't just happen. We don't wake up one morning and discover we have faith. It grows, and the more we exercise faith, the greater is our capacity to live by faith. A story in the life of Jesus helps us understand.

One day Jesus was being pushed and jostled by a crowd.

A woman who had suffered a condition of hemorrhaging for twelve years—a long succession of physicians had treated her, and treated her badly, taking all her money and leaving her worse off than before—had heard of Jesus. She slipped in from behind and touched his robe. She was thinking to herself, "If I can put a finger on his robe, I can get well." The moment she did it, the flow of blood dried up. She could feel the change, and knew her plague was over and done with.

At the same moment, Jesus felt energy discharging from him. He turned around to the crowd and asked, "Who touched my robe?"

His disciples said, "What are you talking about? With this crowd pushing and jostling you, you're asking, 'Who touched me?' Dozens have touched you!"

But he went on asking, looking around to see who had done it. The woman, knowing what had happened, knowing she was the one, stepped up in fear and trembling, knelt before him, and gave him the whole story.

Jesus said to her, "Daughter, you took a risk of faith, and now you're healed and whole. Live well, live blessed! Be healed of your plague" (Mark 5: 25–34).

She lived in a time and place where women were seen as only slightly better than chattels of men. Lacking equity in society, women's access to rabbis was limited, and their significance, especially as determined by religious legalists, was of no account. As well, this woman had a severe medical problem. Her "uncleanness," defined by their laws, meant she must be avoided, for by just touching her, a person would be declared "unclean," which only complicated her life further. That's why any rabbi would go out of his way to avoid her.

But having heard about Jesus, she believed he was her solution. Ignoring the social rules, she pushed through the crowd, deciding to risk everything to get to him. You can imagine her anxiety as she planned to reach out to him. But the problem that had made her life miserable was more than she was prepared to live with. Nothing mattered more than getting to Jesus. In the end her risk-taking faith overcame her hesitation and fear.

THE FIVE-FOLD PATTERN

This second part of our healing journey—walking the road of faith—requires that we understand what is critical to ensure the integrity of our faith. In walking this path of faith with integrity, I see five elements vital to our wellbeing.

HUMILITY

Faith is knowing we can't do it alone. At the heart of faith is humility. We usually come to this point after we've unsuccessfully tried other ways. The woman we've just read about was depleted of all her financial resources and abused by unscrupulous doctors, ending up broke. She reached that low and humiliating moment when she recognized that all the ways she had tried were not enough. In this age of individualism, faith calls us to look beyond ourselves and understand our need.

She took a risk to push past the religious leaders taking up Jesus' time with their harangues, to step around others wanting something from him and to get by his bodyguards, the disciples, who seemed intent on keeping him from being bothered. But she did it. Finally all her life was focused on one thing, and she touched the edge of Jesus' clothes. She had thought about it, planned for it and had carefully positioned herself to be near him. Being a woman plagued by sickness was not going to stop her this time. It was now or never. Her desperate need called for desperate action. She pushed and pushed and pushed. Just when it seemed she would make it, someone would step in her way. In the end, just her finger touched the hem of his garment. But she knew that was all she needed. And it was.

BELIEF

This sick woman needed to believe that Jesus not only could bring her release but that he would. "Yes," she said, "I believe he is who he claims to be and that he holds the answer to my needs." Belief is the

39

assumption that the object of our belief is believable: that is, it can be trusted. If a doctor tells us he understands our problem and has the cure, and his treatment works, we would choose to believe. Believing roots our faith in a reality that has been tested and found to be true. We can then walk this path of faith with Jesus Christ knowing he is both believable and reliable.

EXERCISE RATIONALITY

To exercise rationality is not to say that we rationalize our way out of hurt; it means taking the time to think through what our faith is based on. To bypass the mind is to ignore the very center of our creation. The tendency to ignore the rational side of our nature (especially when we hurt beyond what we think we can endure) rises from associating rationality with stuffy ivory-tower thinking, assuming that the mind is foreign to feeling.

The Apostle Paul directed, "Do not conform any longer to the patterns of the world, but be transformed by the renewing of your mind" (Rom. 12:2, NIV). If you leave the mind (rationality) out of our walk of faith, the path becomes haphazard and idiosyncratic.

In walking the path of faith, we can trust that the scriptural record is historical and accurate. First-class scholarship demonstrates again and again that both the Old and New Testaments can be trusted. So what we know about Christ rises from historical certainty. The story of Jesus of Nazareth wasn't dreamed up, neither are the Hebrew and New Testaments just the clever writings of some desert mystics.

Yes, your mind matters. Don't detach your brain from your self as you walk into a place of worship. Biblical faith requires that we make choices that are thought through. That is not to say that the cognitive or rational mind is the only way we gain insight. But it is to say that our choices need to fit with what we are learning from God's Word and our growing understanding of self.

Clear the Hurdles of Doubt

When we are surrounded by hurt, clearing the hurdles of doubt requires the risk of faith. There are five hurdles to overcome:

1. **"It won't work."** The older we get, the more reluctant we are to take risks, thus preventing us from trying something new. But without risk, we never know what may be. One couple said the reason they decided not to have children was that they didn't know how their offspring would turn out. How true. There is no guarantee how children will end up. But if we believe nothing should be tried because it is not a sure thing, we threaten the possible good which comes from moving beyond our past experience.

2. **"I don't believe in faith."** What a person may be saying is, "faith doesn't exist" or "faith is unnecessary for living" or "faith never works." Faith is not something which exists by itself. It's linked to reality. For example, I have faith in my marriage with Lily. I have faith that the Scriptures are God's word to us. Faith doesn't live suspended in midair. Faith is acting on a premise, believing it will sustain the risk.

3. **"I've never done it before."** The exercise of faith doesn't come easily. Like a muscle, it requires exercise. Some exercise it more than others. As well, some have personalities that make them more inclined to take risks. But this doesn't mean that a more diffident person cannot exercise faith through risk. I suggest that such a person find a counselor or spiritual director to help reflect on the risk. When we hurt we are more vulnerable to making poor decisions. That's why assistance from a trusted person can be helpful as we take steps of faith.

4. **"It might only make it worse."** Yes, that is part of taking risks. However, a few prudent principles can keep us from making it worse: build on a rational foundation; don't grab at the first idea or seeming solution; exercise reasonable precautions; and work with a knowledgeable friend or counselor.

5. **"Maybe if I do nothing, my pain will go away."** That's a lie. Although over time the intensity of the pain will subside, the underlying cause for hurt will not be addressed. When Olive Rogers lost her husband, friend and breadwinner, she had no option but to get a job, no matter what its physical demands. If she chose to do nothing, her family may have broken up and loneliness would have only

added to the hurt. So resist the lie that hurt may go away if you do nothing. Only as your feet walk the path of renewed hope and life-affirming faith will the pain subside.

OVERCOME FEAR

Fear is the antithesis of faith. It immobilizes us. Though fear is a natural response, if it's not overcome, our ability to plan rationally will be hampered, disabling us from executing thoughtful judgment. Fear immobilizes us. At that critical moment we resist fear, we open the window of hope to risk living with God's help. We recognize we can't do it alone, believing that God exists and cares about our lives.

Faith gives us boldness to push past our fears, social constrictions and human interference.

Risk taking is part of the second stage on our three-fold path. When we reach the path of faith we are called to trust the Creator who, as we will see, loves us beyond what we can imagine.

Four

THE WAY OF LOVE

Hope helps us to see with different eyes, faith calls us to risk new ventures, taking us beyond the hurt, but love is that life-force that is at the very heart of our healing. Life without love is barren, self-driven, self-serving and incomplete. We can see with new perspective through a wide-open window of hope. We can move out past the markers by taking risks in the name of faith. But without love, we won't grow.

LOVE IN THE TWENTIETH CENTURY

The past century was a time in which "making love" was redefined. This theme has been the single most sustaining story line of the movie, television, music and publishing industries. We are suckers for equating love with sexuality, even though we know that it is, at best, a shallow definition. Psychiatrist Scott Peck puts it this way: "While I generally find that great myths are great precisely because they represent great universal truths, the myth of romantic love is a dreadful lie."[7]

Darwinian naturalism assumes that life evolved out of some primordial swamp. But where did love come from? Did it also evolve? What was its genesis? In a competitive world, in which the fittest survive, is it only a feeling? Can one think of something which is partial love? If love evolved, what would it look like in a partial state of development? If love is giving for the wellbeing of another, is there something less from which that emerged? Was there ever a "tadpole" of love?

Love is love. It either is, or it isn't. It manifests itself in varying levels of activity: a father will throw himself in front of a speeding car to

43

save his child; a teenager may invite the wrath of his peers by refusing to allow a classmate to be the object of their racism; a woman may remarry her former husband who is terminally ill, to care for him.

The primary framework of our culture has been materialism, which in the end relegates nonmaterial realities such as love to being less than real. The myth (and lie) is foisted on us and welcomed with open arms. No, I must restate that. It would be true to say that Hollywood's version would have had no takers if viewers walked away.

A dominant feature of our culture is that faith has been pushed out of our public discourse. With that has come an increased loss of our understanding of God. It is not a problem of atheism, as few actually believe in no God, but it becomes a problem when worship, faith and belief are seen as private matters only and do not extend to the workplace. When speaking of a colleague who was also a committed Christian, a business friend said, "We have worked together for twelve years, and not once have we talked about what it means to be followers of Christ in business." In separating our faith from our work, we relegate the nonmaterial as being off limits and not vital to our vocational pursuits. Love, like faith, suffers from reductionism.

Though we treasure romance, we know that is only a slice of what love means. I believe that love is central to the essence of the Creator and God of life. What is so remarkable is that, as members of this creation, we too share in the essence of love: loving and being loved. Even though Hollywood has put its spin on the definition of love, we don't have to capitulate and give up on its essence and meaning.

ORIGINAL LOVE

So what is needed? It is a fresh understanding of what the Creator has done in bringing to planet Earth a visible and life-changing expression of love. For us to walk this path of healing, it's vital we come to understand and connect to the life-force of Christ's love.

Jesus got into a discussion about love with a respected Jewish teacher who was curious about the teaching and ways of Jesus. Finally Jesus said, "This is how much God loved the world: He gave his Son, his one and only Son. And this is why: so that no one need be destroyed; by believing in him, anyone can have a whole and lasting life. God didn't go to all the trouble of sending his Son merely to point an accusing finger, telling the world how bad it was. He came to help, to put the world right again" (John 3:16–17).

To understand the dynamic of this love we must understand that Jesus was more than an important rabbi from Galilee, but as the Son of God, he was and is integrated into humanity (in theological terms, he is "incarnate" in humanity).

In the New Testament, Luke offers a prime example of love as God defines it. You'll recognize this story of the prodigal son, but before you assume you know it, take a moment to listen as it would have been understood during Jesus' time, through the ears and cultural mores of that world.

The story begins with two sons and a father with considerable property, which then, as now, indicated a person's importance in the Middle East.

The younger son asks, "Dad, can I have the part of your estate you have willed to me?"

Today that might sound unusual, but not shocking. But two thousand years ago in Palestine, in a culture ruled by fathers, this son was in effect saying, "Dad, I wish you would drop dead." After all, the inheritance would usually come only after the father dies.

To our amazement the father gives him one-third of his estate. The son then plans to leave for a "far-off" city, which in Jewish literature, means a Gentile city. To take his inheritance, he has to sell his portion of the land. The transaction may have proceeded something like this:

The younger son goes next door to their neighbor, Mr. Abe

Suschovitch. After the usual greetings, the young man says, "Mr. Suschovitch, I have some land to sell."

"And what land is that?" asks Mr. Suschovitch. The young man, afraid that he would be asked that question, presses on: "My inheritance, sir."

Mr. Suschovitch is immediately agitated. "Your father has died? But how is it that no one told me of his death? Why didn't you come over and let me know? I would have attended the funeral."

"No," replies the son. "Father is not dead. It's just that I asked for my inheritance, and he gave it to me."

"You mean the land that Moses left Egypt for and Joshua led us across the Jordan for and the land we fought for . . . you mean to say the land your parents and great-grandparents have given their very soul for, you are going to sell it?"

After an embarrassing harangue, a deal is struck, the land is sold, and the young man has his inheritance in gold coins.

Note what has been going on. The young man violated the customs of the patriarchal system and insulted his father; then he took the most precious commodity of the Middle East—land—and sold it; and he is about to leave the land of promise to seek his fortune with the very tribes the Jews fought against to build their land, faith and culture. How much further can he sink? we wonder as the story continues.

In the Gentile city—which suggests a place of ill repute—he loses his money by living a desultory lifestyle. He is such a failure that he ends up feeding pigs. Knowing how popular a ham sandwich is at a kosher lunch, you can imagine what the Jewish listeners of this story were thinking. The young man's life can't descend any further. He is now as far from the faith, customs and land of his people as one could imagine.

Humiliated, hungry and alone, he thinks about returning home. But he has an enormous problem. There was a custom that if a man lost his money to Gentiles or married an immoral woman, the enactment of the *gesasah* would be his fate. The young man knew the townspeople would gather around him, and in a humiliating ceremony, smash a large pot filled with burnt corn and nuts and vent their hostilities on him for having insulted his father and embarrassed his hometown.[8]

As he thinks about returning, the young man invents a story to tell his father. First he will say he has transgressed and is no longer worthy to be called a son. Then what will he ask of his father? The language he chooses is precise: he could ask to be made into a slave, but he rejects that. He could ask to be a house servant, but he leaves that aside. Instead, he will ask his father to permit him to become a skilled laborer. Such a job would allow him to earn his way back into the good graces of his father and therefore his family and community. Over time, with a trade he would be able to earn back what he has lost.

Thus far the Pharisees listening to this story would be pleased, for they had been taught that the only way to gain acceptance by God was to perform works and by so doing, earn their way to redemption. Up to now they would have been disturbed by Jesus' teachings, because he emphasized the very opposite to what they were taught. The story continues.

Because of roving bandits, everyone, including farmers, lives together in the village, protected by the same stone fence and gate. It's evening, and the father is sitting on the porch, drinking his dinner coffee and eating a bagel. He glances over the fence and sees someone coming from the distance. At first he doesn't pay much attention, but as the person gets closer, he notices something peculiar. "No one walks like that except my youngest son," he mutters to himself. As he continues to watch, he realizes the young man really is his son.

As the father sees his son approach, he knows that if the townspeople get to the young man first, he'll be given the *gesasah* and humiliated. He needs to get to him before they do.

But there is a problem: men wore robes, and the only way to run in robes was to lift them. But that leads to another problem: men were not to show their legs. Indeed, in the first century there was a major rabbinical debate over whether a man should lift his robes when walking through thorns. So now what does the father do?

Luke tells us he runs. Children playing in the streets are shocked to see this man of stature running by, holding up his robes, embarrassing himself, all for the purpose of reaching the gate to greet his son before the townspeople. The father arrives, throws his arms around his son, and before the young man can admit his guilt, his father calls for the best clothes and a party to celebrate the return of his son.

The heart of this story is that the father humiliates himself to keep his son from further hurt. Though the son's leaving was his choice and the humiliation was his doing, that didn't matter to the father. When his son turned his steps homeward, the father reached out, accepting him as a full member of the family and demonstrated that by throwing a party. Even though the father had suffered loss and was publicly embarrassed by his wayward son, his response was to love him and by so doing offer new opportunities for him.

This is the nature of our Creator, who shows us understanding and love, offering solutions as we turn our steps homeward.

The Bible's best-known passage about love comes from the writings of the Apostle Paul. Though its rhetoric is without parallel, and it is received as fitting at flowery, lace-adorned weddings, its message cuts across the self-centered mind set of modern culture. In walking the road out of hurt and pain, read it again with new eyes, searching for that which is both consoling and liberating:

If I speak with human eloquence and angelic ecstasy but don't love, I'm nothing but the creaking of a rusty gate.

If I speak God's Word with power, revealing all his mysteries and making everything plain as day, and if I have faith that says to a mountain, "Jump," and it jumps, but I don't love, I'm nothing.

If I give everything I own to the poor and even go to the stake to be burned as a martyr, but I don't love, I've gotten nowhere. So no matter what I say, what I believe, and what I do, I'm bankrupt without love.

Love never gives up.
Love cares more for others than for self.
Love doesn't want what it doesn't have.
Love doesn't strut,
Doesn't have a swelled head,
Doesn't force itself on others,
Isn't always "me first,"
Doesn't fly off the handle,
Doesn't keep score of the sins of others,
Doesn't revel when others grovel,
Takes pleasure in the flowering of truth,
Puts up with anything,
Trusts God always,
Always looks for the best,
Never looks back,
But keeps going to the end.

Love never dies. Inspired speech will be over some day; praying in tongues will end; understanding will reach its limit. We know only a portion of the truth, and what we say about God is always incomplete. But when the Complete arrives, our incompletes will be canceled.

When I was an infant at my mother's breast, I gurgled and cooed like any infant. When I grew up, I left those infant ways for good.

We don't yet see things clearly. We're squinting in a fog, peering through a mist. But it won't be long before the weather clears and the sun shines bright! We'll see it all then, see it all as clearly as God sees us, knowing him directly just as he knows us!

But for right now, until that completeness, we have three things to do to lead us toward that consummation: Trust steadily in God, hope unswervingly, love extravagantly. And the best of the three is love (1 Cor. 13).

When we think of love defined that way, the story of Mother Teresa comes readily to mind, but that of Mark and Huldah Buntain is less familiar. My colleague Jim Cantelon and I were met at the Calcutta airport by a man who Toronto journalist Tom Harpur called "St. Mark." We were assaulted by the humid heat, but we were overcome even more by the human tragedies lining the streets. After some days of walking with Mark and his wife Huldah through the schools, hospital and medical clinics they run, I asked what made them continue here in Calcutta year after year when surely they had earned enough respect from their supporters to return to their native Canada and live out their retirement years in comfort. They were incredulous. I realized that my question made no sense to them, for deep in their lives their desire to give overcame any interest in personal comfort. They had learned to be loving by giving and giving and giving again.

There are three aspects to love: as a verb, as a life force and as a gift.

LOVE IS A VERB

Lily and I were married in her hometown of Kenora, Ontario. Within a few days of our wedding, we packed her belongings and the wedding gifts into our orange 1958 Volkswagen Beetle and headed across the prairies for Saskatoon, where I was attending university. After we settled into our basement apartment, we decided to spend a few days in the mountains of Banff National Park.

As we drove west from Calgary, nearing Cochrane, the mountains were no longer in the distance but rose up on either side. As a boy from the prairies, I'd always thought mountains got in the way of the view, but this day they symbolized something else: my marriage. My goodness, I thought, there is no turning back. There is no way out.

I'm trapped! In Hollywood, love is sentimentalized, built on emotion and good times. But the romantic joy of our courtship, nurtured in the days leading to our marriage, and the delight in now being married, focused me on a new reality: the feeling of love would not be enough to keep us going. We had to will to love.

As we continued in our marriage, I came to see the wisdom of my father's belief: love was what we did, not how we felt. In other words, love is a verb.

Another story from the first century illustrates this. Jesus seemed to find ways of poking holes in the so-called pious legalism of his religious community. One day, coming onto Sychar, a Samaritan village, Jesus met a local woman, and their encounter illustrates the nature of his love, even though he chose to violate community expectations:

Jesus worn out by the trip, sat down at the well. It was noon.

A woman, a Samaritan, came to draw water. Jesus said, "Would you give me a drink of water?" (His disciples had gone to the village to buy food for lunch.)

The Samaritan woman, taken aback asked, "How come you, a Jew, are asking me, a Samaritan woman, for a drink?" (Jews in those days wouldn't be caught dead talking to Samaritans.)

Jesus answered, "If you knew the generosity of God and who I am, you would be asking *me* for a drink, and I would give you fresh, living water." The woman said, "Sir, you don't even have a bucket to draw with, and this well is deep. So how are you going to get this 'living water'?". . .

Jesus said, "Everyone who drinks this water will get thirsty again and again. Anyone who drinks the water I give will never thirst—not ever. The water I give will be an artesian spring within, gushing fountains of endless life."

The woman said, "Sir, give me this water so I won't ever get thirsty, won't ever have to come back to this well again!"

He said, "Go call your husband and then come back."

"I have no husband," she said.

"That's nicely put: 'I have no husband.' You've had five husbands, and the man you're living with now isn't even your husband. You spoke the truth there, sure enough."

"Oh, so you're a prophet! Well, tell me this: Our ancestors worshiped God at this mountain, but you Jews insist that Jerusalem is the only place for worship, right?"

"Believe me, woman, the time is coming when you Samaritans will worship the Father neither here at this mountain nor there in Jerusalem. . . . It's who you are and the way you live that count before God. Your worship must engage your spirit in the pursuit of truth. That's the kind of people the Father is looking out for: those who are simply and honestly *themselves* before him in their worship. God is sheer being itself—Spirit. Those who worship him must do it out of their very being, their spirits, their true selves, in adoration."

The woman said, "I don't know about that. I do know that the Messiah is coming. When he arrives, we'll get the whole story."

"I am he," said Jesus. "You don't have to wait any longer or look any further."

Just then his disciples came back. They were shocked. They couldn't believe he was talking with that kind of a woman. No one saw what they were all thinking, but their faces showed it (John 4).

Jesus was caught in a socially precarious spot: Jews had nothing to do with Samaritans (they were considered half-breeds, a cross between Jews and their old enemies the Philistines); he was talking to a woman, regarded as being beneath serious conversation; and worse, the woman was of questionable character, and Jesus was speaking with her alone, in an out-of-the-way place.

Jesus' love for her was obvious. As much as society viewed her as having no importance, Jesus was concerned about her and helped her grow beyond her experience. In simple terms, he loved her, even though his disciples were shocked by this association. Love calls for that action, even when our contact will create dissonance or misunderstanding. Jesus risked being alone with a person whom society saw as a servant, not worthy of the attention of a rabbi. Love takes us beyond our own interests to people in need.

LOVE IS A LIFE-FORCE

Without love, life grinds to a halt. In reflecting on the nature of the human spirit following his Auschwitz and Dachau ordeals, Viktor Frankl defined love as "that capacity which enables [a person] to grasp the other human being in his uniqueness."[9] The opposite of love is self-interest. If our objective is to serve self, our pursuit of self-interest obstructs the wellbeing of others. The more we live for self, the more we are driven by self. There is a negative self-fulfilling element to those who live for themselves: the more they focus on themselves, the more they are unable to do anything else.

Frankl refers to the Jewish sage Hillel who wrote almost two thousand years ago: "If I don't do it—who will do it? And if I don't do it right now—when should I do it? But if I do it for my own sake only—what am I?" Frankl examines the sage's musings this way:

"If I don't do it—who will do it?"—this refers to the uniqueness of who I am.

"And if I don't do it right now—when should I do it?"—this deals with the unique opportunity which lies before me.

"But if I do it for my own sake only—what am I?"—this suggests I am not truly human at all.

Frankl concludes, "It is a characteristic constituent of human existence that it transcends itself, that it reaches out for something other than itself. To put it in Augustinian terms, man's heart is restless unless he has found, and fulfilled, meaning and purpose in life."[10]

LOVE IS A GIFT

When the apostle wrote, ". . . faith, hope, and love. But the greatest of these is love" (1 Cor. 13:13, NIV), we understand that of all we can pass on to others, the best and finest is love.

As a Christian, I'm interested to note how love seems to be a dividing line between major religions. They separate this way: some see God as that which is outside our human existence and is attained through particular works or rituals. Others view God as one who comes into life and interacts with us. The first grouping has a God we climb to reach; the second has a God who reaches down to human reality.

The Christian faith is based on the latter: the divine takes on human flesh and becomes one with us. The disciple John put it this way:

> The Word [or Christ] became flesh and blood,
>   and moved into the neighborhood.
> We saw the glory with our own eyes,
>   the one-of-a-kind glory,
>   like Father, like Son,
> Generous inside and out,
>   true from start to finish (John 1:14).

C.S. Lewis said a better word for Christianity would be "Lovianity." If there is any gift we receive when we trust Christ, it is love. If there is anything we have to give to others, it is love.

LOVE'S PATH TO HEALING

But why is love so crucial to overcoming hurt and sorrow, and how does it connect as the third leg on the three-fold path to healing? First, hope helps us see that there is a way out of our hurt. Faith calls us to step out and risk. Love brings energy as the life of the divine flows through our attitudes, energizing ourselves, our circumstances and those around us.

The human condition is resistant to divine love, for we are conditioned to believe we have to earn it. "If you want Daddy to love you, you'll have to obey me." The gift of divine love operates differently. We receive it without precondition.

ON THE RECEIVING END OF GOD'S LOVE

When we hurt it's dangerous to assume that the best way to manage our pain is to isolate ourselves from others. If we push open the window of hope and exercise faith, we can connect with God's life-force of love. Wilma Derksen experienced that power of love when her daughter was murdered. Wilma describes their journey in her book *Have You Seen Candace?*

On a Friday in late November in Winnipeg, Manitoba, the prelude to Wilma and Cliff Derksen's nightmare began when thirteen-year-old Candace Derksen called her mom after school to ask for a ride home. Wilma had planned to pick her up, but she hadn't finished cleaning the house, so she asked, "Can you take the bus?"

"Sure, it's okay," said her daughter.

As Wilma worked and waited, the sun dipped over the Canadian prairies, a cold front blew in, snow started to fall, and with it, the temperature. Wilma knew that Candace wasn't dressed for this rapid turn in the weather. So with a growing sense of panic, she took her younger children in the car with her to find Candace. "We crawled along the back lane and then drove along Talbot Avenue as slowly as the rush hour traffic would allow. I glanced in the windows of the 7-Eleven store, the neighborhood hangout, but she wasn't there. The further we drove, the faster my heart started to pound. Where was she?"

In desperation Wilma drove to Cliff's office and told him she couldn't find Candace. He grabbed his briefcase, and as they walked to the car, she quickly filled him in on the details.

At the car they looked for a moment at each other. Wilma said, "There is something to be said for fifteen years of marriage. Not every thought has to be voiced to be understood." Once in the car, they both tried to appear calm for the children's sake. She continued, "I could see that all my fears had been transferred to Cliff's eyes. We were of the same mind. It should have been a comfort, but it wasn't."

They looked everywhere and called anyone remotely connected with their daughter. No one had seen her. Finally at eleven o'clock, police officers dropped by to interview them. Wilma remembers that the officers still seemed skeptical, having seen numerous thirteen-year-olds run away or stay out over night without telling their parents.

The police took a picture of Candace and promised to put out a city-wide alert. Days stretched into weeks. Christmas and New Year's passed with no celebration. Seven weeks after they started the search, the police finally found her body in a shack just blocks from home, frozen, with her hands tied. After the autopsy had been done, two detectives gave Cliff and Wilma the details. Wilma describes that moment:

> After we had made sure the children were occupied, we sat down in the living room. Very carefully the detectives set the scene. Candace had died of exposure—hypothermia, they said. The toxicology test indicated she had not been drugged or poisoned. All they knew was that someone had tied her hands and feet and abandoned her to die in the freezing temperatures. The crime scene was disorganized; it looked as if someone had attempted to bury some of her belongings, and as if this person had spent some time with her.
>
> Even as we sat there listening, the whole situation seemed so unreal, so totally illogical; this couldn't have happened to our family. This wasn't the kind of thing that happened to peace-loving Mennonites living in Winnipeg.
>
> My need to know dragged me back to reality. "Was she sexually assaulted?" I asked.
>
> "No."
>
> "Was she hurt in any way?"
>
> "No."
>
> But why? we asked over and over. None of it made sense. Why would anyone take a young girl and tie her up and leave her to die? What could the motive have been?
>
> The police shrugged their shoulders and watched our reaction as if they were waiting for something. They gave us a few more details and said Candace's vocal chords hadn't been swollen. She hadn't tried to scream.

Oh, God! She hadn't screamed! Who had terrorized her so completely that she hadn't even screamed for help?

"It doesn't look as if she struggled much," they said, and continued giving us details.

No struggle could only mean that she had been too scared, too terrified, I thought. She must have thought it too hopeless or dangerous to try. They concluded, "We feel because of this evidence that she was probably with someone she knew."

I couldn't believe it. The police had arrived at a totally different conclusion than I had. No struggle and no screaming spelled terror to me, but the police thought it meant a lack of fear. I tried to explain, but they couldn't seem to fathom anyone not fighting back—a perspective probably based on the difference between being a woman and being a tall, well-built male, I realized. . . .

Another part of me, the 10 percent that doubted everything and had been hurt by the accusations that she had run away and had wondered about all the sightings and all the different interpretations, that part needed that bit of information. It laid all doubts aside. It was conclusive evidence that we had known our daughter. She really had been an innocent little girl—half woman, half child—who had been lured or forced off the street and terrorized. We had known Candace, and it was wonderful to have her memory secured.[11]

Candace had died before she could even begin to live. Instead of a beautiful, white wedding dress, her parents had to buy a cold, white coffin. "Would I ever be able to accept the injustice of that?" Wilma wondered.

A year later, on the anniversary of Candace's disappearance, Wilma struggled with guilt and anger: guilt over failing to press the police to send out their dogs and anger at the murderer and then at the police. In her struggle for relief from her anguish, she wrote, "I couldn't really forgive my daughter's murderer. It would be a vicious circle. I could try to forgive, but who could ultimately wipe this guilt away, throw it into the deepest sea? Who could bear this guilt and rage?"

In struggling to find someone to help her, she realized it had to be "someone who was part God, because God was part of the tragedy, and someone who was totally innocent, because Candace had been innocent in her death." Her resolve turned her to faith. "And there in the shadows I saw the cross. Better than ever before, I understood why Christ had to die. I'll never really understand the mystery of what happened on Calvary, but, at that moment, I finally knew where I needed to go with all of the guilt."

And she did. She recalled, "The deadness was gone. I was again free to enjoy all the beautiful memories we had of Candace. I could again remember the love, the goodness, the beauty of her life. The memories were no longer framed by guilt."

When the force of God is brought into our lives, we feel the power of his love.

LOVE LIBERATES ME FROM ONLY SEEING DEATH AHEAD

Adam and Eve, our original parents, disobeyed God's instructions for them in the Garden of Eden: "You are free to eat from any tree in the garden; but you must not eat from the tree of the knowledge of good and evil, for when you eat of it you will surely die" (Gen. 2).

Death became the inevitable outcome of life. Try as we might to avoid it, we can't. When a loved one dies, the sense of loss is enormous. When you wake up in the morning without your spouse next to you in bed, or your Mom is not there to see you off to school, or your daughter will not be calling home from college, you dread facing the day. God's love expressed in Christ helps remove the sting from death. It helps us see past physical death to a life beyond, lifting that paralysis that keeps us from seeing anything but death.

Nicholas and Claire Wolterstorff lost their son Eric in a mountain accident. In *Lament for a Son* he writes:

> I stand before the library, where he spent so many days of his last months. He's walking up these steps, through these doors, to the desk, asking for a book, receiving it, sitting down at the table—which one?—copying out these notes I have.

No, I see nothing; no form at all, not even a trace. All bone and muscle gone, the steps swept clear—no smile, no sturdy step, no bright intelligence, no silhouette, no love embodied. Where he should be, I stared through.

Turn it back. Stop the clock and turn it back, back to that last Friday, that last Saturday. Let him do it over: get up late this time, too late to climb, read a book, wait for his brother. Let him do it right this time. Let us all do it right.

It won't stop; it keeps on going, unforgiving, unrelenting. The gears and brakes are gone. There's nothing I can do to make it stop. Farther back and farther yet, back into the dimming past. The gap begins to gape.

Is there no one who can slow it down, make it stop, turn it back? Must we all be swept forever on, away, beyond, beauty lost, and love, sorrow hard on sorrow, until the measure of our losses has been filled?[12]

Nothing can fill the void. No words will cool the heat of sorrow. No memory will ease the gut-aching loss. Nothing. There is no way but to allow sorrow to wash over our conscious and unconscious being. Eventually God's love breaks in, at first like a flickering candle, reminding us that all is not lost. Nick Wolterstorff concludes with thoughts about the afterlife:

I don't see how he's going to bring it off. But I suppose if [God] can create he can re-create.

I wonder if it's all true? I wonder if [God is] really going to do it?

Will I hear Eric say someday, *really* now I mean: "Hey Dad, I'm back"?

"But remember, I made all this, and raised my Son from the dead, so . . . ."

OK. So goodbye Eric, goodbye, goodbye, until we see."[13]

In the pain of death, dying is not the end.

LOVE HELPS TO LIFT THE SENSE OF GUILT

Nothing induces guilt quite as much as suicide does. On one hand, we recognize that the person was so overtaken with hopelessness that the only way out seemed to be to end his life. Yet those left behind are now robbed of any opportunity to bring closure to their own sense of responsibility. In the end, the guilt remains.

I asked my sister-in-law Evelyn how she dealt with her guilt after the loss of her daughter Jill. She replied:

I'm sure it's no surprise to know that I did have guilt. I wasn't a perfect mother! A lot of "should haves" flitted through my mind and escaped my lips. I should have told her more often that I loved her. I should have noticed some signs of depression. I should have given her a special card, instead of waiting for the right time. I should have called her that evening. And the list goes on . . . . The nagging thoughts of not meeting your daughter's needs can be devastating.

Working through guilt doesn't come instantly; it's ongoing. But I remembered positive incidents that happened over the years and especially the summer of the year she died. She had been working as a lifeguard at a camp and seemed discouraged one day when she called. I wrote her a long letter, reminding her of many fond memories of the family, and at the end of the letter, I told her how much I loved her.

I remembered sitting in the hospital emergency room that summer; she was waiting to see a doctor about an eye infection before returning to camp. It was a time of sharing and just being together.

I remembered arriving home Thanksgiving Sunday, just after we learned of her death and there was an unwrapped gift and card she had bought for our anniversary.

Also I reach out to young people in their needs and feel empathy and compassion for them. Sitting with grieving parents and sharing a common bond gives me courage and strength to ease the guilt of my own failures.

I know that if Jill were to stand before me today, she would extend love and forgiveness to me. And I know I would open my arms and say, "I love you and forgive you." All guilt would be gone—*Forever!*

Love Calls Us to See through Clear Lenses

Rage and anger do the opposite. They are blinding, so we can't see ourselves or others. The Apostle Paul said in his moment of rebirth, it was as if scales fell from his eyes.

Love Opens Us to Truth

Love helps us learn what is true by pushing aside what is self-serving, even at personal cost.

Love Calls Us to Do What is Right

Love and justice have great affinity. The lens of love corrects our inclination to see only what we want to see. Love helps us see what is, which in turn, helps us do what is right. We live with two kinds of sin: the sin of commission—we do what we should not do (the Ten Commandments make that clear); the second is the sin of omission —that is, failing to do what we should do. While attacking a person is wrong, it's just as wrong to not respond to a victim's plea for help. Love acts both as a stimulus to do good and as a retardant to keep us from doing wrong. Love is powerful, calling us to go beyond our self-interest. The way of love is both the source and means of health.

HEALING BY GIVING LOVE

If you drive south from Israel's palm-lined city of Jericho into the desert, you will soon see a large body of water some five miles wide and forty-five miles long. It looks inviting and pleasant as viewed from the western hills or from eastern Mount Nebo, where Moses looked out onto the Promised Land. But, saturated with salt, this lake has no life. Nestled between the Moab Plateau on the east and the hill of Qumran on the west, this is the Dead Sea.

What's so remarkable about the Dead Sea is not its location but that it has continued to exist over thousands of years. The surrounding terrain is desert and could well do with irrigation, but this sea has no ability to help. Though the Jordan River flows into it from the north, there is no outlet. That's why it's dead: it receives fresh water but gives none. As the Dead Sea continues its intake of fresh water from the Jordan River, the more it needs to sustain its own level, even though it gives nothing away except by evaporation. No fields are fed. No one drinks from its supply. No birds ride her waves.

What a contrast to the Sea of Galilee (actually a lake), some miles to the north. It nurtures fish, irrigates fields, is a feeding ground for birds and satisfies the thirst of those who drink from it. Unlike the Dead Sea, it gives as much as it gets. From the southern end of the Sea of Galilee, the Jordan River begins its southward flow, blessing the valleys it passes through, all to end in the lifeless Dead Sea.

This is the picture of life without love: life trapped into self when the flow of love is cut off. Without the life-force of love, we become its opposite: like drinking salt water, a lack of love only produces a greater thirst. When I "love" in order to get pleasure, then pleasure is the best I can expect. But if the object of my love is other than self, then life is enhanced, whether I get pleasure or not.

Earlier we recalled the story of the prodigal son. But there is a tragic side to that story. While the father was extravagant in how he expressed his love to his wayward son, how different it was for the son who stayed at home. He still would receive his share of the inheritance. That had not been lost. Through the years of his younger brother's wandering, the father continued to offer his older son love and security. Yet with the return of the younger brother, the elder sulked and withdrew, offering no love to his brother or father. He complained that, even though he had been faithful and worked hard on his father's farm, no party had been given in his honor.

What he failed to see was that the good things given by his father were always his. The gift of the father's love was his every day. Yet he didn't recognize that love because he himself was not giving. He may have thought his father loved him because he was faithful. If he had only realized that he too could have known the personal experience of his father's gift of love as his father had shown his derelict brother. The gift of love is received only when given away.

One year after that fateful Friday night when Candace disappeared, Wilma Derksen was asked how she felt. She recalls feeling that capital punishment would not have been enough for the person who had taken her daughter and tied her to her death. For Wilma, "Ten would have to die and I would have to pull the trigger. I felt good when I said that to myself. It would take that much justice."

Wilma had been working with Lifer's Program, designed to take parents of a murdered child into prison and meet with a convicted murderer. Called "surrogate dialogue," it provided an opportunity for parents of a victim to confront someone who had killed. René Duroche, himself an ex-convict, supervised the program and worked to help both victimized families and convicts reach some sort of inner resolution through this dialogue.

René detected that Wilma had not dealt with her anger, and that by helping other families she was only covering up her inner anger. He decided to turn the tables on Wilma and arranged for a meeting for her. Wilma told me her story:

We went to the Stony Mountain Penitentiary where René had hand-picked a group of men with whom I would meet. We all agreed we would be totally honest. I knew some of the men, others I didn't. There was a mixture of races, some were gang leaders, others included a teacher, accountant and artist. I asked them their full names (they'd often refuse to give their last names) and their status as a convict. In that moment I knew I needed to know why they had killed, who they had killed and what led up to that moment of killing. I pushed them to set aside their typical rationalizations and tell me honestly. And they did.

As they told me their stories, all of a sudden I realized I didn't need to kill any of them. In that moment I was beyond my anger. Then I noticed something I hadn't picked up on: there were ten men. That image I had of finding justice by personally pulling the trigger and killing ten men lifted as I had just spent time with ten who were of the very type I had fantasized killing.

I learned compassion—not to ignore the need for justice—by seeing others' humanness. This group of ten later in conversation agreed this was a first-time experience for them. They felt as if I could look right through them. It was also a moment of accountability; their defenses were down. One said it was as if I was like God, telling them how I felt about them. It was during this encounter I began to understand their anger because I too understood rage. That time became an intimate moment of truth. As strange as it seems, we became friends and felt the impulse to hug. I knew their souls, and they knew mine. It was something beyond being male or female, but of recognizing each other's pain.

The power to love comes from hearing the story of the perpetrator, not to excuse or absolve, but to understand and in understanding to love. The action of sitting and asking questions and listening is an act of loving. Setting aside the impulse to judge—or as in Wilma's case, setting aside her fantasy about pulling the trigger and killing ten men—puts one in the place of having to listen and to even possibly understand.

For Wilma the healing really only took full effect when she began to love the very kind of men who might have killed Candace. The built-up anger, kindled by her fantasy of pulling the trigger, was cleaned out by the fast flowing river of love. Rather than ending in a sea of death, she allowed the flow of love to work its way through the lives of those she had despised. It was then that healing was hers.

In leading us toward healing, what does love do?

LOVE PULLS US OUT OF OURSELVES

While we're hurting, the last thing most of us think about is loving someone else in need. Our hurt is so consuming that we rush to fix it first. While pain focuses attention on self, love does the opposite by drawing our attention away from ourselves.

One day Dave and Evelyn learned of a family in our community whose eighteen-year-old son had taken his life. Within hours they were there to give love and understanding. Who can better look into the hurting hearts of parents who have just learned that their son or daughter has committed suicide than those who have been there? Out of their own grief, they found that loving others not only brought hope to those in grief but provided respite in their own lives. Nothing brings health like loving another.

Lillian Marshall discovered a new world after her husband died. She had been active in her community, and she and her husband had operated an insurance brokerage for years in the maritime community of Moncton, New Brunswick. Now on her own, she wondered what would fill her life. One day Lillian's minister asked if a woman coming from the west to visit her son in Dorchester, a maximum-security prison some miles away, could stay with her. She welcomed the visitor to her large house. Before the mother left, she asked if Lillian would see her son, as there was no one else to visit him.

Thus Lillian began an odyssey of caring for young men trapped in the violent world of a maximum-security prison. What made her special was not only her loving, outgoing nature, but her life experiences. As a mother, she knew children. And age was on her side; she could care for male prisoners without having to worry about sexual conflicts. As much as she grieved at the loss of her husband, she let herself use her nurturing skills to care for men in need. What a gift!

LOVES CLEANS OUT THE IMPURITIES CLOGGING THE ARTERIES OF OUR SPIRITS

Loving others has a way of cleansing our lives. One of the most valuable words of counsel I received in seminary was that when we were hurting, we should make hospital calls. It was more than comparing my state to the condition of the patient; by the very act of loving and caring, my life was renewed.

After Jill's death my brother David sold most of his business interests and did what he had always wanted to do: help the poor. I recall some years earlier sitting around a campfire in Algonquin Park in northern Ontario. Our boys were asleep in the tent and we were talking around the camp fire. He was in a struggle of faith. In the conversation he told me of the impact Bob Pierce had had on him while in high school (Pierce had founded World Vision, which cares for people in need around the world). Dave recalled how struck he was with this person of faith who also deeply cared for the poor. Out of this boyhood memory, Dave discovered his own love for people immobilized by desperate circumstances. He describes the importance this work has had in his own healing:

> Five years or so before Jilli left us, I had begun to fulfill my dream of working in the developing world. I had spent time in Bangladesh, the Philippines, Thailand and West Africa. I closely associated each case with the poor and with the refugees in Thailand. Their plight bore deep into my soul, and I was profoundly touched by their ability to cope with the worst that life could dish out. Early in our new life (after Jill died), I was reminded that most of the poor that I had met were grieving parents. When that realization hit home, I felt that I had joined a very special fraternity. Some of the areas where I visited, the statistics indicated that up to 40 percent of the children had died before reaching the age of five. Imagine the pain. About eight months after Jilli's funeral, I visited one of the areas in Mali, West Africa, and as I met each of my brothers in the Dogan tribe, they held me with a tenderness and moaning that underscored my membership with them. Who was I to walk a road that did not share with them the particular pain of losing a child?
>
> As I began picking up the pieces after the death of Jilli, I visited other areas of the world experiencing grinding poverty. I found that each encounter ripped open the wound again. My uncontrollable tears and moments of sobbing became a personal embarrassment, and I thought that I would have to give up this side of my life. I could accept the pain, but the physical manifestations were awkward. A breakthrough came during a Sunday service in the mountains of Sumatra when a group of women stood up in the service and sang a

song in their language with a melody that took me back to my child-hood: "Make me a blessing to someone today." The dam broke, and I was able to mix my tears with joy as I continued my resolve to work among the poor.

LOVE GOES BEYOND MY OWN ABILITY TO LOVE

The middle-aged couple sat across from me, their eyes trying to find a place of comfort, but finding none. They had asked to see me privately. I wondered what could be so distressing. Their marriage seemed happy.

After a few moments of background, the husband finally blurted out, "We just found out that our son is gay." And with that he began to sob.

"Where in the world did this come from?" he finally asked, after regaining control.

We talked for an hour, during which time it became obvious they dearly loved their son. But they felt that with their Christian view on the matter of a homosexual lifestyle, they had no choice but to cut off their ties with him. We went back to their love for him. After some coaxing they agreed to work on loving, and not judging, him.

Some months later we met again. After our last meeting, they had worked harder at spending time with their son and left aside the subject of his lifestyle, unless the son raised it. They continued to express their love for him, even though people in their church found out about his choice to live with his partner.

Now much later they had learned what it meant to love, to continue to show that he was still their son and that, even though his lifestyle clashed with their views, they respected his choices. They not only discovered how their love reconnected the bonds of family, they found they could also love his friends.

Love does that. It reaches past our heartbreaks into the lives of others without condemnation or rejection.

When we love, we draw on the ultimate source of love. God's reservoir becomes our own.

Five

WHEN CRISIS COMES

Scott Peck opens *The Road Less Traveled* with, "Life is tough." We all know the heartache of missed opportunities, the sense of failure in relationships, self-anger over what might have been and regret over mistakes. We will all feel wounded sometime in life. This refutes myths that "we can have it all" and that life should be good. When we experience pain, we know this isn't true.

Easy times and happy circumstances are not the norm. Just as life seems to happily roll along, something breaks in. We can't assume that good people doing good things are going to have good times. God doesn't hand out credit cards with the promise, "Here, take this and have a good day." To live requires risk. There is no obvious logic as to why some people breeze through life with hardly a scratch, and yet those who push beyond the borders of self-service and give their best for the wellbeing of others often seem to get hammered.

The ancient story of Job is a classic tale of a good man made to suffer. Not only did his life come crashing down, but he couldn't figure out why it happened. It's one thing to fail and understand why it happened, but it's quite another when life falls apart, your business goes belly up, your children and grandchildren die, you are covered with sores, and you have no logical explanation for this monstrous calamity—now that's psychological dissonance!

Job was wealthy, powerful and very successful. In the ancient Middle East, wealth was measured by cattle, flocks and family. In financial terms Job was the Bill Gates of his world.

The story opens with God conversing with his angels, when Satan breaks in. God comments to Satan that one of his servants, Job, is as good as they come.

"Oh, come now, we all know why he is so good," Satan replies. "You've been protecting him. No wonder he is such a nice guy. Look at his incredible wealth—where did that come from? All you have to do is take that away, and he'll curse you to your face. I can bet on that!"

"Okay," says God, "you can take a run at him, but under one condition: don't lay a finger on him."

Satan does what God permits. Within days Job's cattle are stolen, his sheep destroyed by lightning and his camels run off by thieves. Servants die, and a tornado sweeps across the plains and smashes the homes of his children and their families, killing them all. Job is now living in poverty without even a roof over his head.

What does Job think? Remarkably, he bows and worships:

Naked I came from my mother's womb,
    and naked I will depart.
The Lord gave and the Lord has taken away;
    may the name of the Lord be praised (Job 1:21).

God asks Satan, "Have you considered my servant Job? There is no one on earth like him . . . And he still maintains his integrity, though you incited me against him to ruin him without any reason" (Job 2:3).

"Skin for skin!" Satan responds. "Back off completely and I'll show you what he's made of."

So Satan is given free rein, with the caveat that Job's life be spared. Within days another catastrophe strikes. Job is covered with itching sores from head to foot. His wife asks, "Are you still holding on to your integrity?" She offers her only recorded advice: "Curse God and die!" With that Satan slips from the scene, not to be heard of again.

This story is the backdrop for a major conversation. As Job sits in ashes, scratching himself and bothered by his questioning wife, his friends arrive to offer him their counsel. History has sarcastically labeled them "Job's comforters"—and not for nothing.

To the question of "why," these three friends are simplistic in their views. They assume that the reason Job has lost everything and is in pain is that he has done wrong. The way they see it, only the guilty suffer. Job is suffering; therefore, Job is guilty. But Job disagrees. Until he finds out what wrong he has done, he isn't going to cave in to their presumptions.

As the dialogue continues, Job decides that the only way he is going to get to the bottom of this is to put the question to God, face-to-face. He wants to know why this suffering has come to him.

In biblical accounts, God never appears visibly. He speaks with a voice like a whirlwind, sweeping away everything in its path. But instead of answering Job, God lambastes him with two hard questions: "Where were you when I created the world?" and "Who do you think you are to demand that I explain who I am to you?"

Job is stunned. There are no further arguments to be made. God makes no effort at all to soothe Job's hurting heart. There are no answers for his questioning mind. There are no gentle metaphors to quiet his troubled spirit. There is nothing.

Our reaction might be to call the whole thing off and walk away. We might say, "If God doesn't have at least a smidgen of sensitivity to give me some sort of answer, then I'll get on with my own life and forget we even talked." Not Job. He sees there is no reason why he should be exempted from suffering. Job came away from this encounter with new insight, knowing that fighting God is counterproductive. His health and wealth were eventually restored, and he became more successful than before.

This story teaches us much about the issue of hurt. There are some things that come our way over which we have no control: A downturn in the economic climate comes seemingly without warning. The government decides to downsize education, and as a teacher you don't survive the cut. You lose a contract to someone else for no apparent reason. A tornado reduces your house to matchwood. The company you work for is run by the very best of managers, but new technology costs you your job. Lou Gehrig's disease takes your spouse in mid-life. A gang of thugs bursts into your house, terrorizing you, robbing you, vandalizing your home. There are all kinds of reasons for disaster, many of which have nothing to do with us, and yet are hurtful to our lives, families and community.

What are we to make of it all? Job tried to see beyond the circumstance of his own downward spiral. Try as he might, he couldn't make sense of it all. Even the advice of his consultants shed no light on the darkness of his soul. Which way to go? What to believe? Who to trust? These questions plagued his mind.

There comes a moment in our search, after we have examined possible factors contributing to the crisis, that we must back off and leave aside our attempts to figure it out, admitting there are some things beyond our control and beyond our comprehension. This does not mean we capitulate. We must not assume there are no answers. It's just that we have come to an edge of human existence where we should recognize that our knowledge is limited, that true understanding lies beyond the darkened glass.

MAKING CHOICES TO SURVIVE

There are still choices to be made, however. To be caught in the web of living as a victim will only suck us further into the morass of self-pity and disability, be it emotional or physical. Out of his Auschwitz experience, Frankl observed that,

The experiences of camp life show that man does have a choice of action. There were enough examples, often of a heroic nature, which proved that apathy could be overcome, irritability suppressed. Man can preserve a vestige of spiritual freedom, of independence of mind, even in such terrible conditions of psychic and physical stress . . . . Everything can be taken from man but one thing, the last of human freedoms—to choose one's attitude in any given set of circumstances, to choose one's way. . . .

In the final analysis it becomes clear that the sort of person the prisoner became was the result of an inner decision, and not the result of camp influences alone. Fundamentally, therefore, any man can, even under such circumstances, decide what shall become of him— mentally and spiritually.[14]

Most of our personal experiences are not of such heroic proportions. Those whose life-stories stand on our bookshelves likely didn't plan to become heroes either. It came out of the courage and determination not to assume that life is a free ride. Though we all hope that life will deal us a good hand, when the time of pain comes, as Frankl notes, we all have the choice to decide how it will affect us. The enormous capacity of the human spirit to make choices is a gift too often written off.

The school of behaviorism defines the human personality as being a function of material properties. Personality is crafted, so the theory suggests, by physical realities, thus causing us to behave in a mechanistic way. The comic Flip Wilson made famous the line, "The devil made me do it." This resonates with many who feel that we have no control over what we do. The Apostle Paul looks at this inner struggle of the human will: "What I don't understand about myself is that I decide one way, but then I act another, doing things I absolutely despise. So if I can't be trusted to figure out what is best for myself and then do it, it becomes obvious that God's command is necessary. But I need something *more!*" (Rom. 7:21–22).

Even though we struggle with good and evil, we shouldn't begin with the assumption that we have to give in to our pain. Healing starts with making the choice to move out from our hurt.

LIFE INVOLVES DEATH

The cycle of life begins with death. As much as we would want it to be otherwise, death is essential to life. There is no other way for wheat to multiply but to go through the cycle. I grew up on the prairies and recall watching a farmer looking out over his frozen fields in winter. With all that possibly could go wrong before the grain was sold and the cheque was in hand, why take the risk on such odds? First there is the spring: Will it be too early? Too late? Will we get enough rain— or too much—for the seed to properly germinate? Then during the growing time, will there be enough moisture—or too much—to bring it to full head? And what about disease, grasshoppers and such? Then at its ripened best, can the crop be harvested before late rains or early snow, which would downgrade its quality? When it's in the granary, what price will we get? Is there a glut on the market, or is there a high enough demand? These questions flood a farmer's mind as he surveys the windswept, snowy plains in mid-February.

All these risks notwithstanding, as a kernel of grain undergoes the rotting process, its coat drops off. Without that, the germ of life will die. But through the destructive process of stripping off the exterior shell, the journey of reproduction begins. That germ, when exposed to soil, extracts from its new environment what it needs to grow. More than that, it is called on to grow. For within its genetic code is an impulse which drives it on its way to becoming a new generation. Jesus said, "Unless a kernel of wheat falls to the ground and dies, it remains only a single seed. But if it dies, it produces many seeds" (John 12:24, NIV).

Hurt occurs when our external protection is stripped away; security is gone, and the interior is exposed to death. To what degree is this stripping away the beginning of a new journey or the end? That is the question for which we require an answer.

While there is within each of us the resilience to overcome inner injury and hurt, the value of such pain can be accessed when we

73

understand that, just as the grain "dies" to create new growth, the loss of our own protective shell is the beginning of the next part of life. As difficult as it is to see beyond our hurt, death brings opportunity for newness. The self can be multiplied beyond what it ever would have been. This happens as our interior germ reaches out to new sources of life.

SURVIVORS

Once a painful crisis strikes—whether from events beyond our control or as the result of our own action or failure—the only control we have is our reaction to the hurt. Here are some lessons from those who've made it through financial and career crises, survived personal failure and overcome the hurt of personal loss.

BLOW UPON BLOW

To know Gerry Clemenger is to be loved. Lily and I met Gerry and her husband Jim while involved in a national youth ministry. They were so loving and encouraging to us.

After being raised in a divorced home, Gerry met and married Jim. They had three children. Their marriage was loving and seemed like a storybook romance. But life would not always be so happy. Jim experienced severe financial setbacks in his business. It went into receivership, and in order to pay their business debts, Jim and Gerry had to sell their home.

"I remember moving out of our lovely five-bedroom, ravine home in Toronto and moving to a rented home," Gerry recalls. "I consoled myself with the thought, I could be a widow and be moving because my husband died. At least I have a husband."

Then four years later on Father's Day, Jim died of a heart attack. She told me:

> I didn't expect to be a widow at fifty-three. When the doctor said Jim wasn't going to make it, I was shocked. I remember thinking, "I can

live three weeks without him." I knew that, because once he had been away for three weeks, and I seemed to get along. We had had many challenges in our marriage, and yet Jim was always there to support me. He never raised his voice. He treated me beautifully. He was nine years older than I, and I think that because I didn't have a father, Jim became my security.

After his death, I cried every Sunday for eight months. I thought I would never get over it. I was surrounded by wonderful friends at our church, who continued to include me in their plans. I thought I was doing well, but a close friend said it would be five years before I would be my own person. I recall once at a party I laughed, and someone said, "There is the old Gerry." But death changes you. You are never the same again.

Then, within five years, another tragedy struck while Gerry was visiting her daughter Juanelle, her husband Steve and their three children in Alberta. Juanelle, a nurse, was driving home after working the night shift when she fell asleep at the wheel, and crashed. "I recall answering the door and a policewoman was there," Gerry remembered. "I invited her in. 'Has my daughter been in an accident?' I asked. 'Yes,' the policewoman replied. She then asked me to sit down. Holding my six-month-old grandchild, I sat down. 'Is she dead?' I asked. 'Yes,' was the numbing reply. For the next year and a half I cared for the children. I thank God for the privilege of doing that, because it helped me work through the grief by having something tangible to do—to take care of the grandchildren I so dearly loved."

Then, in a relatively short period of time after the funeral, her son-in-law fell in love and decided to remarry. To Gerry it seemed too fast. Yet she knew her grandchildren needed a mother and Steve needed a wife. Gerry pushed on, convincing herself of this, yet struggling with the thought of "a woman other than my daughter in the arms of my son-in-law; someone other than my daughter being called 'Mommy' by my grandchildren—it seemed almost too much."

Through the deaths of her husband and daughter, Gerry continued to pray, "Lord, I open my hand. I accept your will. I don't like it, I don't understand it, but I accept it."

Then life took on a new twist. One day she received a call asking her to be a dorm parent at the Black Forest Academy in Germany, a boarding school for children of missionaries in Europe. Her real assignment was to be a "grandma." She asked why she was being invited to fill that role. They replied, "We watched you with your grandchildren when they didn't have a mom, and we think that when these young children cry for their mothers, you'll know how to comfort them."

As wonderful as the idea seemed, Gerry wondered, "Suddenly I saw the biggest 'Why' in my life. I saw that my deep pain could turn out to be a tool of ministry. I thank God for my other children, Betty Anne and Bruce, who encouraged me. But I almost got caught in playing it safe. After the two deaths, I had found a job in Canada I really loved. The people were great to me, and I was good at what I was doing. I also had a nice apartment. I had just bought a new car and thought, Here I am, a woman at the age of sixty-four. Should I be taking that kind of risk?"

However, at retirement age, Gerry decided to take the risk. She left Canada and moved to Germany. When she made the decision to leave family, friends and her newfound security, and move to a land she had never visited, little did she know the joy that would be hers.

In the meantime, Steve and his new wife Audrey had moved to Hungary. Gerry was thrilled when she was invited to spend Christmas with them and her grandchildren. After finishing her assignment at the academy, Gerry returned to Canada to take up her life again. But soon another call came from the academy, asking her to return. When Gerry agreed to return to Europe, she contacted Steve and Audrey. She was in for a surprise. Steve said, "You'll never believe it, but we've decided to send our children to the academy!"

"So here I now had my own two grandchildren in my dorm, tucking them into bed," said Gerry. "When I heard that Jonathan and Stephanie were going to be there, I just envisioned Juanelle running in her exuberance to Jim my husband in heaven and saying, 'Daddy, you can never believe what's happening on earth! My kids go to the school where Mom is.' I can't believe that in all of this God gave me the privilege to love and care for my grandchildren."

In retrospect she reflects on her sorrow:

Being from a divorced family where my dad left me when I was six, I'm amazed at how often, when I am tucking the children into bed, they will ask, "Grandma, were you ever away from your parents?" Though I can't tell them the heartache of a being a little girl and having a daddy who doesn't come home to tell me he loves me, I am able to look into their eyes and say that their mommies and daddies love them. What a wonderful privilege.

Grief really is about adjusting to live your life alone. It takes a long time. I often feel like I am on the edge of a precipice, looking into a fog as I'm about to take the next step. The next step is one more year, but beyond that I don't know.

As I look back over these fourteen years, I can see how God unfolds the future.

Gerry discovered that freedom is more than financial. It's found in living a life of hope, faith and love. Drawing on her life experience, she is able to love, nurture and comfort children separated from their parents. Her tragedies and sorrows flow out into a loving stream to nourish lonely, young children away from their parents and home. Her risk of faith opened the river of love.

SURVIVING THE ECONOMY

Pekka Varvas is one of hundreds of thousands of people riding the roller-coaster economy. I first met him when, as a young, commercial artist from Finland, he was building his career. On Wednesday mornings we'd meet at a local restaurant for early-morning Bible study. I watched as he and his wife Anita built their life together in Canada.

In 1981 Pekka left a large advertising agency and, with two colleagues and a secretary, launched a new advertising business. In the boom years, Pekka saw his partnership thrive. With close to forty employees and an annual business income of over $5 million, he felt he had finally arrived. His lifestyle reflected his financial success, including expensive vacations and investments.

Ten years later recession hit. Money that had been easy to earn was no more. Suddenly, clients couldn't pay their bills, and Pekka and his partners found themselves accumulating bad debts.

The partners eventually had to put the company into bankruptcy, with Pekka carrying liabilities close to $1 million. The bank repossessed his assets, and he was forced to file for personal bankruptcy. He reviewed the situation, made adjustments and set up Varvas Marketing Communications with one of his former partners. But this too failed when one of his major clients declared bankruptcy two years later. While he dealt with his creditors again, his cash-flow reserve was wiped out. Though he didn't go bankrupt, he was forced to close his business. A year later he formed a new agency.

In reflecting on the past, he said, "It's easy to become self-reliant when money is rolling in. Your priorities get messed up quickly and easily." Pekka accepted the first business failure as God's way of dealing with him and giving him the perspective his life was missing. "Maybe I wasn't ready to operate a business of that size," he muses. "When things started going badly, I refocused my priorities. I had to evaluate what was really important. I had a wife who still loved me and devoted kids and a heavenly Father who loved me."

The second time around he had a more difficult time. He was angry with God. "The second time I had been working hard on doing it right. I was balancing my time with my business, family and Christian service. I was blind-sided by what happened. I was emotionally hurt and totally lost confidence in myself at that time. I felt like a failure."

He recalls his source of strength during those painful days: "During the darkest days, my wife gave me a verse from the Bible for each day. What a strength it was to see me through the tough times. A favorite was 'For I can do everything with the help of Christ who gives me the strength I need' (Phil. 4:13)."

CORPORATE SHAKEDOWN

Jim and Faye Boehmer know the rough-and-tumble world of corporate life. At thirty-nine Jim headed the Canadian subsidiary of the world's largest biscuit company. From there he became president of a food-processing company in a large multinational corporation. Did he enjoy his work? "I certainly did. And I did well. During my three-year tenure we increased sales by 66 percent and profits by 2.6 times."

Life was going well. Outside his work he contributed as a volunteer in the community. Both he and Faye were involved: Faye taught a Sunday-school class, Jim served on church-finance and education boards, and both were part of weekly Bible-study groups. Jim had also been on the executive of a group arranging for one of Billy Graham's visits to Toronto.

But at work appearances proved deceiving, as he was soon to learn. "It all came crashing down. Called to meet with the chair of the company, I was expecting to be given an additional bonus; I was given my walking papers. The real reason emerged after about two years. I had put a stop to a practice that, up to then, had been an accepted part of doing business. However, I saw it as morally wrong, and something I couldn't endorse."

Jim said that people in the human resources field call this type of dismissal a lack of fit. "I obviously didn't fit when it came to values and principles. But why me? The company was growing profitably and my wife and I had never been so busy in the Lord's work. Though one is not to be repaid for efforts to honor God, surely God's work would have been furthered by my being the successful president of a company. How could further failure advance the cause in any way, I wondered."

Today Jim helps men and women make vocational transitions, an ability based on his skills and experience, something that didn't come easily or without hurt. A colleague said, "Jim Boehmer has helped more people in the jungle of business in downtown Toronto than he'll ever know. His understanding of men who struggle with ego and being successful in our modern business climate comes out of his own search for success and meaning in the hurts of business leadership. He knows what he's talking about. His personal faith integrates with what he does."

GIVING IN THE MOMENT OF PAIN

My scientist brother Dr. Calvin Stiller—whose groundbreaking work at the University of Western Ontario has been recognized worldwide in the medical revolution of organ transplants—tells how the giving of life can lift one up from experiencing an abject sense of total loss into remarkable joy in giving the gift of life:

One evening a car full of teenagers was driving down a country road. A runaway horse raced along in a ditch parallel to the car. Without warning the horse jumped from the ditch and landed on the hood of the car. The horrific result: a perfectly healthy eighteen-year-old man had his neck broken and was rushed to intensive care at our hospital, suffering trauma that led to his death.

I wanted to ask the boy's family about possible organ donations. I accompanied the young resident neurosurgeon to the quiet room of the intensive care unit, where the father and mother were sobbing. I spoke gently to the father, asking him when he had last seen his son alive. The father was guarded and somewhat hostile. After a few moments, he answered my question. He told me that, as his son left home with his classmates, they had said goodbye, the father offering some last-minute advice about driving. Looking forward to a day in London with his classmates, his son had driven off.

I then broached the difficult topic of donation. "When you came in to see your boy today, I know you were shocked to see his head bandaged and his body still and unconscious. But what gave you hope as you stood by his bed, was that when you touched him, his skin was still warm. You placed your hand on his wrist and felt his pulse. You looked at the cardiac monitor, saw the tracing and heard the beep. You also heard the swish of the respirator and saw his chest rise and fall. All of this convinced you that life was still there.

"However, a brain tracing has confirmed the fact that your son's brain is not injured or asleep, not bruised or damaged, but irrevocably dead. Your heart cries out that this can't be so. Your boy is exactly the same as when you first saw him here at the hospital. But your reason affirms that it is just as the specialist has told you. Your son is dead and will never recover. Reluctantly, you have accepted the facts. You know it is time to turn the respirator off. You want to take your son to the funeral home and from there to his final resting place.

"But even now the signs of life remain, because there is an enormous amount of life remaining in your son's body. We used to define death as the cessation of heartbeat. Now we know that organs die at different rates. And the brain dies long before many of the other vital organs do. So, as long as the heart is maintained, life in the organs after a fatal injury is exactly the same as it was before. In fact, with the aid of a respirator, the heart could function for some time.

Then the father asked, "Dr. Stiller, are these real patients who will get the organs, or is it all just for research?"

I told the grief-stricken parents the other side of the story. "Upstairs on the sixth floor is a woman twice your son's age. She is dying a slow but sure death because her liver has failed. The same problem applies to a young man living in this city. His heart is slowly ebbing away. He wears a pocket pager, waiting for a call saying that a new heart is available."

I paused to focus my thoughts, and then continued, "I would like you to be a key participant in this wonderful retrieval of life."

I felt the atmosphere in the room change. The meaningless destruction of a healthy teenager—having healthy organs but brain dead—could be transformed into something meaningful after all.

The father grasped his wife's hand. "Dr. Stiller, can you promise that's what will happen?"

The next day the boy's parish priest called me. "May I tell those who will be attending the funeral what has happened?" he asked.

"Yes," I said. "Tell them a thirty-six-year-old woman facing death is going to live because of a new liver. A forty-one-year-old man can look forward to a future because of a new heart. Two patients who were tied to artificial-kidney machines are being released from their prisons. Two people who could not see the sun rise in the morning will receive sight. A child suffering from third-degree burns is receiving new skin. And a young man will have a joint transplant and walk again. All this because these parents were determined that the death of their son did not have to end only in tragedy."

Several weeks later, the boy's father wrote: "I've lost my son, but I take comfort in the knowledge that somewhere out there a part of his life goes on."[15]

CAMBODIAN HORROR

Sometimes we can understand how love can rise up to ward off evil. But in this story about Reaksa, I'm astounded by the power of this young man who learned, out of incredible pain, what it means to go on.

It was 1977. The Khmer Rouge, under the infamous Pol Pot, was in power. Eleven-year-old Sokreaksa "Reaksa" Himm remembers the soldiers arriving in his village of Seamreap with the instructions that everyone was to get in the government trucks, destination unknown. His father was skeptical, but they had no choice. The family of thirteen, including the oldest son's fiancée, walked to the school where they were told to board the trucks. As Reaksa was about to toss his bag of clothes onto the truck, a soldier pointed a gun to his head and said, "Drop it."

"I thought at first he must be joking, but he wasn't. He looked very angry. He kept the gun on me. When I realized he meant to shoot me, I was both terrified and angry. Our confrontation seemed to last for minutes. In my terror I could not seem to act. My father and sister screamed at me to give up the bag. I was every bit as angry as the soldier, but I was powerless. I dropped my bag and jumped on the truck."

With other families—all educated people—they were shipped to the jungle, where they were forced to build shelters and survive on rice and salt. Any resistance was met with being "sent to study," the chilling phrase for being shot.

During the next two years, they were forced to perform various kinds of hard labor. Reaksa's mother suffered from bouts of malaria; his father was forced to help destroy a Buddhist temple, which was a form of spiritual torture for him. Also a baby brother and a nephew were born. At times starvation was a very real threat. Then his older brothers were sent away, never to be seen again. At one point Reaksa's ten-year-old brother, accused of stealing corn, was hung on a fence, beaten to unconsciousness, aroused, beaten again, then dragged through the village. Later an older brother, also accused of stealing, was forced to confess, then was tied to a stake outside all night without a shirt, leaving him to the torture of the mosquitoes.

Eventually Reaksa, his father, his younger brothers and his sisters were dragged outside the village to a pit. His father was clubbed and thrown into the pit. The children were ordered to kneel by the grave. Reaksa felt a blow on the back of his neck and fell on top of his father, followed by his brothers and sisters. He recalls the numbing sensation as their blood trickled down on him. The soldiers stepped into the grave, hacking up the bodies of his family. They hit Reaksa again, but still he lived.

Because they were going to bring more people to be executed, the soldiers left without filling in the grave. When they were gone, Reaksa disentangled himself from the bodies and hid in the jungle. As he watched the soldiers march in the next batch of victims, he saw his mother, older sister, sister-in-law and nephew among them. He watched helplessly as they too were killed and thrown into the pit.

For a time Reaksa survived alone in the jungle, eating what he could find. When he dared to return to his home village, one man endangered his own life to look after him. But again Reaksa had to hide for his life as this foster father was pressured to take him into the jungle and kill him. For another four months, he survived alone in the jungle.

Some four years later, the Vietnamese armies drove the Khmer Rouge soldiers from his area, allowing Reaksa to return to his village, collect the bones of his family and bury them at a Buddhist temple. From there he went to live with an aunt, but had difficulty coping with life. In a Buddhist society, his pain was viewed as the natural consequences of karma, the law of cause and effect—he was reaping what he had sown in earlier incarnations. As an older teenager, he joined the police force, an opportunity, he thought, to get revenge on the Khmer Rouge soldiers who had so devastated his life. "I was hungry to suck the blood of those who murdered my family. I fantasized in detail about my revenge. I longed to torture them and cut them into pieces. Revenge was my only reason to live." Finally, when the opportunity came to kill the soldier who had ordered his family's execution, he found it impossible.

In 1984 Reaksa escaped to Thailand, first as an illegal refugee and then for five years under official United Nations High Commission on Refugees sanction. It was in the camps that he encountered Jesus Christ. After five years in a refugee camp and hearing about the Christian God, he prayed, "Lord God, I have been hurt enough. I cannot carry my life by my strength any longer. I am tired of life. I need your help. I want to go to Canada. If I am accepted to live there, I will believe in you." Six months later Immigration Canada accepted him. He flew to Canada and was sent to the World Vision reception center in Toronto.

As liberating as that moment was, it was not the end of Reaksa's suffering:

> Though I did not understand it at the time, I had developed the
> characteristic symptoms of psychological distress: reexperiencing the

traumatic event, guilt about having survived while my family perished, about not being able to help them. I experienced anxiety-depressive manifestations, flashbacks, repetitive nightmares, irritability, a tendency to aggressive-violent behavior, emotional numbness, cognitive construction, psychosomatic features and a generally lower level of adaptive functioning. I could not remember what I tried to learn. I could not remember what I said to friends. I could never remember what I did. Frequently I became restless. I could not stay in one place or do the same thing for very long.

I was damaged in the basic structure of the self; normal ways of thinking and feeling and the usual ways I had handled stress in the past were disrupted. I lost trust in myself and in others. My capacity for intimacy with others was damaged by intense and contradictory feelings of need and fear. I was unable to have loving feelings. I did not know who I was. I felt lost.

Over the years Reaksa has found some answers to his questions. "Since I lost my family under the brutal Communist regime in Cambodia, one of my greatest desires has been to search for the meaning of pain. Why is there pain in this world? People who have gone through suffering find hope in many different ways. My own experience of struggling with the issue of suffering has led me to become a Christian and to find a new hope in Jesus that gave me courage and strength to walk through the fire of pain."

Reaksa is currently working on his Ph.D. in clinical psychology, with plans to do his thesis research in a Cambodian hospital and then to work with Cambodians suffering from the wounds of war. "I want to see Cambodian people start to smile again. They have suffered so much, and nothing will make them whole again except the healing message of Jesus' love and forgiveness."[16]

Six

IF GOD KNOWS, WHY THE HURT?

The haunting loneliness of sorrow is made worse when we pose the question, "If God knows, why the hurt?" Asked throughout the ages, it persists with few satisfactory answers. If the person asking the question believes there is a God, it opens the discussion. If, however, the person doesn't believe there is a God, then there is no point in pursuing an answer. To make sense out of this question, indeed even to continue, we must begin with the premise that God exists.

You'll note that the stories in previous chapters had two common elements: hurt and personal faith. Belief in God doesn't mean the pain is any less, rather it's that those who believe in a personal God have the capacity to feel the hurt within a larger framework of meaning. It isn't that for Christians the "why" is more easily answered or even that they find a satisfactory answer. But viewing the hurt within a more cosmic perspective provides a place for the question as one seeks the path of healing. If the landscape of our questioning is wide, we have more opportunities to see the question from a variety of positions. However, it all begins with the premise that God exists.

A BACKGROUND

Where did God go in our culture? Throughout the latter part of the twentieth century, the collective acknowledgement of a personal God in the Western world has diminished. Through much of the twentieth century, public debates have increasingly declined to recognize

86

God as integral to human life and society. As we tie our vision of life to material wellbeing, as fewer and fewer people participate in prayer, Bible reading and church attendance, we've lost the capacity to turn our sights outward when grief, hurt and despair take hold. For example, in a recent funeral at Peggy's Cove, Nova Scotia, on Canada's east coast, in memory of the hundreds who lost their lives in the Swissair crash, the protocol officer of the Canadian government instructed the Protestant and Roman Catholic ministers not to use the name Jesus Christ or to read from the New Testament. This is symptomatic of how we've shut off Christian faith within public spheres.

We are living in a world in which the very idea of knowing God has been made by some not only unfashionable but unspeakable. The lasting impact of this trend has been to privatize faith so that faith becomes what is believed or practiced in the confines of a church, synagogue or mosque. To understand that this has happened is critical, for if in our public places we say, in effect, there is no God, despair becomes real for many. For the past century, we have seen this encroaching paralysis rob us of the grand understanding that a loving God does exist.

German philosopher Friedrich Nietzsche defined the radical reshaping of what academia would teach when, at the turn of the twentieth century, he pronounced, "God is dead." For him God had become meaningless, irrelevant to his beliefs and thinking. The combination of Darwinian naturalism, along with optimistic humanism, "dismembered the carcass of a comprehensive world and life view which had upheld man for centuries."[17] The sense of being alone in the universe, which is prevalent in our post-Christian world, only heaps despair on despair.

Nietzsche's notion became not just an idle idea—that we in modern civilization no longer needed to believe in the existence of God—but said that God no longer lived. God was not just irrelevant; he no longer existed. In 1889 Nietzsche told this parable:

Have you not heard of the madman who lit a lamp in the bright morning and went to the marketplace crying ceaselessly, "I seek God! I seek God!" There were many among those standing there who didn't believe in God so he made them laugh. "Is God lost?" one of them said. "Has he gone astray like a child?" said another. "Or is he hiding? Has he gone on board ship and emigrated?" So they laughed and shouted to one another.

The man sprang into the midst and looked daggers at them. "Where is God?" he cried. "I will tell you. We have killed him—you and I. We are all killers! But how have we done this? How could we swallow up the sea? Who gave us the sponge to wipe away the horizon? What will we do as the earth is set loose from its sun?"[18]

Nietzsche asserted that the strong ought to triumph over the weak and exploit life for their own purposes. With no vision of truth or morality in such chaos, man is taken over by the superman (Nietzsche's word). Though he didn't have in mind the Nazi form of superman, he viewed the world as having no moral compass. His ideas, in turn, shaped those of many thinkers and influencers of the twentieth century. What emerged was not only a loss of active Christian thinking in education and the media, but a growing sense of despair in the broader culture. The reason this shift in thinking matters to our concerns is that in moments of hurt and grief, if there is no one we can turn to, nor a framework in which we can face our pain, we are indeed hopeless.

During the early part of the twentieth century, the Third Reich took Nietzsche's ideas—twisting and distorting them to be sure—and built their malicious schemes in a moral vacuum. How prophetic were the words of Russian writer Feodor Dostoevsky: "If there is no God, then everything is permitted." Nietzsche's atheism went beyond intellectual search and became political, as he had intended. He wrote, "I am not man, I am dynamite . . . my truth is fearful; it is that in the past we called lie the truth—the devaluation of all values. . . . The concept of politics is completely taken up in a war of the spirits, all the structures of power are blown up into the air, for they are based on the lie. There will be wars of a kind that have never happened on the earth."[19]

And how right Nietzsche was. Within years the two world wars of the twentieth century blew apart romantic Western notion of humanism.

In his book *Night*, Elie Wiesel, a survivor of the Holocaust, recounts his boyhood and the herding of his village into cattle cars headed for the prison camp of Birkenau. The description of those moments is quite impossible for most of us to imagine. He writes, "Never shall I forget the smoke. Never shall I forget the faces of the children, whose bodies I saw turned into wreaths of smoke beneath a silent blue sky. Never shall I forget that nocturnal silence which deprived me, for all eternity, of the desire to live. Never shall I forget those moments which murdered my God and my soul and turned my dreams to dust. Never shall I forget these things, even if I am condemned to live as long as God Himself. Never."[20]

I find particularly striking what Nobel laureate Francois Mauriac writes in the foreword to *Night*:

> It was then I understood what had first drawn me to the young Israeli: that look, as of a Lazarus risen from the dead, yet still a prisoner within the grim confines where he had strayed, stumbling among the shameful corpses. For him, Nietzsche's cry expressed an almost physical reality: God is dead, the God of love, of gentleness, of comfort, the God of Abraham, of Isaac, of Jacob, has vanished forevermore, beneath the gaze of this child, in the smoke of human holocaust exacted by Race, the most voracious of all idols. And how many pious Jews have experienced this death! . . .
>
> Have we ever thought about the consequence of a horror that, though less apparent, less striking than the other outrages, is yet the worst of all to those of us who have faith: the death of God in the soul of a child who suddenly discovers absolute evil?[21]

The Holocaust, shaped by Nietzsche's superman ideology, reminded the world we had taken another step on the path of despair. This growing sense was aided by the writings of French authors Jean-Paul Sartre and Albert Camus. In Sartre's world humankind is left on its own, operating out of a notion of freedom in which life has no reason: no reason to be born, to marry, to pursue a vocation, to love, to hate, to care for or snuff out the life of a child or to live or take one's own life. Herein is the agony and despair of freedom in a world in which one is the author of one's own choices. In such a world of unbounded and uninhibited freedom, there is no knowledge of good and evil, there is nothing that is right or wrong, good or bad, better or best. Here is the terrible anguish: one has to decide for the whole world, without any basis for the decision.[22]

In an appropriately titled novel *Nausea*, Sartre describes how meaningless life is: "Nothing happens while you live. The scenery changes, people come in and go out, that's all. There are no beginnings. Days are tacked on to days without rhyme or reason, an interminable, monotonous addition."[23]

Given there is nothing significant for one to do, he writes, "'I was just thinking,' I tell him laughing, 'that here we sit, all of us, eating and drinking to preserve our precious existence, and really there is nothing, nothing, absolutely no reason for existing.'"[24]

In 1957 Albert Camus was awarded the Nobel Prize for Literature. The citation states that this award was given because "of his important literary production, which with clear-sighted earnestness illuminates the problems of the human conscience in our times." His "clear-sightedness" is expressed in his three novels *The Stranger*, *The Plague* and *The Fall*. Camus' attempts to show how people actually live and make sense of life in a world without God. While for Camus it was important for humans to do what is right by opposing evil and to help alleviate suffering, morality exists in a world without God, who as creator has continuing oversight over creation. At the heart of his writings there is a despair: one seeks to live a moral life in a world in which a moral order exists but cannot be defined. In *The Fall* he concludes that, in the absence of God, a substitute is required, even if that substitute is slavery: "Ah, mon cher, for anyone who is alone, without God and without a master, the weight of days is dreadful. Hence one must choose a master, God being out of style."

Even though Camus affirmed a sort of morality in life, C. Steven Evans writes, "He refuses to admit that everything is permitted, and searches vainly for a way to become a saint without believing in God. In a world where 'God is out of style,' Camus becomes for us a prophet of despair."[25]

NO ANSWER WITHOUT GOD

So how are we to deal with the question, "If God knows, why the hurt?" If we assume, as did Sartre and Camus, that we live in a world without God, then God is not a factor, and the question is moot. Even if we agree with deists that God exists and has spun creation into existence then backed away without any involvement, we end up the same as if we believed there were no God, for with a deistic God, there is no human engagement, concern or involvement. An agnostic view—that there might be a God, but one can't be sure— also keeps us from going on. We can philosophize, looking for answers, but it ends up as intellectual game playing.

The truth is, I can't offer you hope without God. Without God, I have no idea how one can find inner healing. Not only is it absurd to think of life as being the result of fortuitous chance, but to appreciate the complexity of human life in all of its beauty and conundrums, without God, is to take a leap of faith beyond credulity.

Our question assumes a map that points us to a path of healing. But there is no promise of easy answers, for great minds and hearts have wrestled with this question for centuries. To those caught in grief, there are no solutions that right now, in this moment, will lift the pain. It is rather by way of our journey that we come to understand that our queries are not readily answered and our concerns are not quickly solved with either simple or complex theories. Healing will be ours, but it will come in time and as lessons of life are learned.

QUESTIONS TO ENABLE US IN OUR SEARCH

There are two important questions we ask in our journey out of pain: Is hurt evidence that God doesn't care? And why does God allow hurt?

IS HURT EVIDENCE THAT GOD DOESN'T CARE?

Philip Yancey begins his best selling book *Where Is God When It Hurts?* with a reminder that pain is not a bad thing; it is not a blunder that, if God had a second chance, he'd leave out. We assume that pain is abnormal and, therefore, something to be avoided. If we fall into the trap of assuming that pain is, in and of itself, something bad, then when we experience hurt, we conclude God doesn't care.

In an earlier book *Fearfully and Wonderfully Made*, Yancey tells the story of Dr. Paul Brand observing his patients in a leper colony in India.

One day, to his horror, he saw a member of the leper colony reach into a fire to retrieve a lost potato. To his amazement the person showed no signs of discomfort. Trying to learn more, he followed some of his patients around. One day a young, emaciated patient noticed the doctor was having trouble turning a key in a rusty lock. He pushed up alongside Brand, took the key and opened the lock. Dr. Brand knew it took a great deal of force to open the rusty lock and wondered how this leper could have done it. It was then he noticed blood dripping from the lad's finger. Taking the boy's hand in his, he examined it and saw that the flesh of his index finger had been broken open by turning the key. Yet the boy showed no discomfort, just like the patient he had seen a few days before putting his hand into the fire.

Brand decided to examine more closely how the disease of leprosy actually worked. The conventional medical wisdom had been that leprosy was a kind of fungus eating up human tissue, so that fingers and toes, for example, would fall off. In his research Dr. Brand, now recognized worldwide for his pioneer work, discovered that leprosy attacks the cells that produce pain. So the cells that would warn a person of impending danger were, in effect, dead. Therefore, the lad had no warning that by turning the key, he would break open the skin on his hand. The mechanism of pain that would have alerted him and prevented this violation wasn't alive to tell him.

Yancey describes visiting Brand in the Louisiana leper hospital where he conducted research and treatment. A patient Lou was almost blind, blind because of no pain. The microscopic cells on the surface of his eyes were dead and unable to signal that there was irritation that, in turn, should trigger the eyes to blink. As the eyelids blinked less and less, his eyes gradually dried up, leading to blindness.

Yancey concludes, "Pain is not an unpleasantness to be avoided at all costs. In a thousand ways, large and small, pain serves us each day, making possible normal life on this planet. . . . Without pain, we would lead lives of paranoia, defenseless against unfelt dangers."[26]

To recognize the important role of pain in protecting self is not a clever way to dismiss the matter of emotional pain. Though we are more focused on the personal, inner side of suffering, the analogy of physical pain is not something we should ignore. C.S. Lewis reminds us that "pain insists upon being attended to. God whispers to us in our pleasure, speaks in our conscience, but shouts in our pain: it is His megaphone to rouse a deaf world."[27] This "megaphone" serves as a reminder that something is wrong. In that sense pain's value is that it awakens us to the underlying reality.

One day, some years after the death of Jill, my brother Dave and I went for a boat ride out from the cottage he and I had purchased years earlier. As I was moving some of the life jackets, a child's life jacket turned over and there written on the back was "Jill." Dave looked at me, and we both wept. As tears rolled down our faces, we headed across the lake to a bay, turned off the motor and drifted in the breeze. We talked about the recurring pain. "Do you think it will ever end?" I asked.

"I don't know," he said slowly. "It has changed and will change even more, but this pain is important to me for it reminds me that the daughter I so deeply loved is gone. I don't want to forget that." The reminder is not disabling, but it does keep in mind that that one person so important to his sense of life is now gone. This continuing pain—albeit at increasingly lower levels of intensity—in turn, sensitizes both him and Evelyn to the heartache of others.

Pain then, as a megaphone, should not cripple, but empower. In the opening days and weeks of such a loss, the pain will, of course, be crippling. But such pain is natural, for it tells us that our interior construct, which gives us the capacity to love in the first place, is intact. Now that the loss is staring us in the face, we shouldn't cut off our emotional ties to the person who has been with us in a relationship of joy.

Human emotions hurt when we press on them, just as a thumb hurts when it's hit with a hammer. It is part of God's loving arrangement to get our attention. Otherwise, we would continue on our way without being warned. For Brand, pain is a great gift from God. I recall him saying, "Thank God for inventing pain! I don't think he could have done a better job. . . . Only dead people don't hurt."

Pain comes for various reasons. Some we bring on ourselves in the normal course of living. When we overwork, irritability warns us that we've pushed our limits. If we violate a criminal law, the punishment of the court tells us we've crossed the legal line. When we discard our marriage vows, family turmoil may result. If we cause death by reckless driving, our grief will linger as we remember the life we've snuffed out.

Pain also comes because of what others do. If gossip damages our reputation, we know the hurt of being misrepresented. For adults who were sexually abused as children, the seething sense of violation causes untold pain. When our employer goes bankrupt, the loss of a job upsets our sense of productivity and being able to provide, and that hurts. If a spouse walks out, our self-image is battered, and life may go into a tailspin. If a child is killed by disease or an accident, the ongoing sorrow will be sustained in our memories and in the lost hope for his future.

Whether we hurt out of self-inflicted pain or by grief brought on by another, the warning signs of hurt are a gracious gift from God. If we felt nothing, that would indicate a lack of ability to even care in the first place. We can't have tender feelings for another and then feel nothing if we lose that person. We can't have one without the other. God has woven into the fabric of our lives the capacity to feel, care and become attached. We aren't made to live as islands. We are born out of the warmth and security of the womb. Our first moments are at our mothers' breast. Helpless, we rely on parents to raise us. We live within relationships as we were intended. When those connections break, hurt is a natural result of being disconnected.

WHY DOES GOD ALLOW HURT?

If our ability to experience pain is evidence that God cares, why does he allow those things which cause hurt in the first place? Can't he at least prevent things that cause hurt and have no apparent purpose? To ask it in other ways, "Why doesn't God keep bad things from happening, such as my child dying of a disease?" or "Why doesn't God order the world so that natural disasters don't destroy it?" or "Why doesn't God keep people from doing things that hurt others?"

Both Judaism's and Christianity's understanding of this basic question comes from the Hebrew Scriptures, the Old Testament. It begins this way: "In the beginning God created the heavens and the earth" (Gen. 1:1). We aren't told what kind of God he is or how creation came about. The story unfolds, showing the progression of creation, one event upon another. Then human life comes. First it is man, then as the Creator notes, it isn't good for man to live alone, so woman is created. The two are given responsibility for overseeing the garden in which they lived.

There are three things to note: First, God alone created everything. There is nothing other than God; there are no other gods, no creation to which God is subservient. Life came from his will and that alone. Then after creating the cosmos, God saw that it was good; there was no evil in this creation. Third, human life is unique in that it bears the image of its Creator. Though animal and plant life were also seen as good, only the human being was stamped with the likeness of the Creator. The *imago Dei* became the special part of creation. As well, humans were called upon to participate with the Creator as stewards of creation. In the harmony and balance of creation, human life carries out the will and concern of the Creator.

In their assignment to husband creation, humans are told that one tree is not to be accessed. That tree provides humanity with an understanding of the difference between good and evil. And if they know that, they are warned, evil will intrude into their lives. Therefore, they are to have nothing to do with the tree. In the course of time, the serpent speaks (which does not seem to surprise either the man or woman), subtly convincing them that to eat of the tree is to their advantage. They argue that the Creator has said that if they do that they will die. The serpent disagrees and eventually convinces them of his point of view, and they take of the fruit. In that moment "the eyes of both of them were opened, and they realized they were naked; so they sewed fig leaves together and made coverings for themselves" (Gen. 3:7).

They now know why they had been warned. In their embarrassment they become self-conscious of their exposure. Taking leaves, they sew together garments, symbolizing the radical shift in their sense of self and how that related to the environment and their Creator.

That afternoon the Creator arrives for his daily visit, but the man and woman are hiding in the trees and God calls out to them, and the man responds, "I heard you in the garden, and I was afraid because I was naked; so I hid."

God's response is telling: "Who told you that you were naked?"

Then the man and woman tell the story of what they've done. The man blames the woman, and she lays blame on the serpent. From that breaking of the relationship between the created and the Creator comes the upheaval of both creation and human life. The devastation of that disobedience breaks the harmony of creation and humanity, pitting one against the other, and changes the relationship of God to creation. John Milton sees it this way: "It was from out the rind of one apple tasted, that the knowledge of good and evil, as two twine cleaving together, leaped forth into the world. And perhaps this is that doom which Adam fell into of knowing good and evil, that is to say of knowing good by evil."

Living on this side of that cataclysmic break, it is hard to grasp its vastness. Humans entered a different phase when they disobeyed God, losing their purity and intimacy with the divine. What was natural became an embarrassment. Not only did they hide from each other behind the covering of leaves, but they tried to hide from God in the trees. The resulting impact was global. The man and woman were set at odds with creation. The Fall violated the principles established under creation. The principle of shared resources was turned upside down. Resources became objects of greed and envy. The powerful hoarded rather than shared. Instead of care for the environment, abuse and pollution became accepted standards. God's human creation came to oppress others and their environment.

That is the world in which we live. Pain exists and, as part of continuing creation, we seek refuge from it, wondering what life would be like if it had never been introduced.

So is God, therefore, bound to maintain that condition? Given that God is God and is able to do as he wills, why doesn't he simply do away with it?

Rabbi Harold S. Kushner, in *When Bad Things Happen to Good People*, attempts to resolve the problem of pain. Out of his own sorrow for his son, whom he watched die of the disease of progeria, Kushner concludes that, while God is loving, he is simply unable to do anything about it, as he points out in the chapter "God Can't Do Everything, But He Can Do Some Important Things." He concludes that, as much as God wants to do what's right, he is not all powerful. Kushner's problem is that, in attempting to preserve God's reputation, he compromises our hope in a God, who by his power assures us that a time is coming in which sorrow and hurt will be no more.[28] The flaw in his argument is that to support a God of love and yet cripple him by claiming he is not all powerful, is to end up with no God at all.

What kind of person did God create? Were humans created to live as automatons, in automatic obedience to God's imposed will? Or was this creation—*imago Dei*—given the freedom to make choices? We know that the first humans did not know the difference between good and evil. As Professor Stackhouse reminds us, "We must understand Adam and Eve to have been created in a state of innocence, not in a state of moral perfection. The former means they started with a clean slate, with no disposition to do wrong. They could, however, choose evil at any moment."[29] In brief, they were given free will to make their own choices, even if those were outside the expressed instructions of the Creator.

Three factors unfold from this premise:[30]

1. First, because God is the creator of all and nothing happens without his allowance, God is responsible for everything that goes on. This is made clear in the prophecies of Isaiah: "I form the light and create darkness, I bring prosperity and create disaster; I, the LORD do all these things" (Isa. 45:7). God allows events to occur even though he doesn't bring them about. We don't know why God allowed moral disorder to enter into human race. We begin, however, with the premise that he did.
2. We know that human creation was given the right to make moral choices. Free will allows us to say yes or no to the Creator. That the God of all life would allow man, in whom he endowed his likeness, to move outside of his boundaries is remarkable. Was it because he wanted his human creation to have the ability to choose to serve and love the Creator? We don't know. All we do know is that it happened. We find within the wide sweep of the two testaments an extraordinary relationship that develops between people and God. This ultimately finds its fulfillment when God integrated with human life itself in the person of Jesus of Nazareth.
3. Finally, in the course of civilization, humans have defied the Creator time after time. Instead of opening our lives to his gracious love and provision for doing grand and wonderful things, we resort to our own puny ideas, and by so doing, bring about disasters of all kinds. We violate our marriage covenants and generate hurt, anger, distrust and brokenness. We rob virtue from our children and wonder why they end up dysfunctional. We greedily encroach on our neighbor's land and end up in bloodbaths. We exploit our oceans and wonder why fish decline to the point of extinction. We drive recklessly and cause loss of lives. We violate the integrity of other races and then deplore racism and conflict within our cities. By the way we (mis)conduct our lives, we deny that God exists, and yet in moments of hurt and pain, we cry out for his help.

When we awake to our need for healing, we realize we haven't developed skills to help us think about and speak with the Creator. From the accumulation of evil upon evil, hurt upon hurt, we stumble along, living for ourselves, all the while going upstream against what God has for us. This flaw, called "original sin," we inherited, so that even as I look into the smiling face of my newborn grandson Pearson, I know that as much as this tiny being is innocent and uncorrupted, he too "caught the bug," the flaw of that first sin, accumulated over the centuries. There will come a time when Pearson will be faced with making a choice between serving the self-interests society says are natural or in humility serving his Creator. But that will be his choice.

So what is the Creator to do when those made in his image choose to walk outside the prescribed borders? If you were God, what would you do? There are four possible solutions for God: he could end it all, remove human free will, perfect all of life now, or give it time.

Yes, God could end it all. There are moments when we wish life were over. I confess that some years ago in my malaise, I looked at older people with envy. The world had lost its interest. While I'm the kind of person who loves challenges and enjoys taking risks, my vision, dreams and plans then seemed like sawdust in my mouth.

Indeed, God could wrap it all up now. But as evil as the world is, as flawed as I am, as hurt I am today, it is better that I'm alive. Stackhouse picks up on philosopher William Hasker's suggestion that "(a) if I do not regret my own existence nor (b) the existence of those whom I love, and (c) if my own existence and the existence of those I love depends on the previous existence of a long line of ancestors, all of whom sinned, plus (d) a global history of troubles that doubtless influenced my family tree and the ancestry of those I love, then I cannot condemn God outright for allowing any evil, or even a lot of evil, in God's administration of the world."[31]

Peter Kreeft points out that within the wider question of human existence, it is better that God not end it all. "You haven't committed suicide. You've decided, for whatever reason, or even for no reason, to live. . . . In the middle of the story that is your life, are you glad you're in it? You've answered yes by choosing to stay alive. You must believe you have more pluses than minuses in your life, because you could always move to zero, but you don't."[32]

We could also ask, "Why not take away our free will so we would, without even having to think about it, do good?" To remake and remove free will would take away the very essence of what it means to be made in the image of God. We would lose the ability to make choices, and to walk freely in communion with God. If humans were forced to love and serve God, in the end there would be no true communion.

Another course would be for God to perfect life now. With some waving of the wand, God could—we propose—make hurt and pain disappear. However, underlying the dysfunction of life is something more basic and systemic. The flaw in human life and civilization is the real issue. Dr. Brand learned that leprosy is not the decay of flesh but the loss of feeling. That is the core reason for hurt. If God then were to deal with the symptoms of our malaise, it would require radical surgery on our very nature.

That's the very point! God is moving history to that ultimate time of perfect rule. The entire Scripture reverberates with his loving and determined plan to bring us into a time and place where "sorrow will be no more." From the time of our original parents, that plan has been in force. Indeed, the very steps to healing are found as we open our lives. As God changes our human will, we'll take the path leading to a world where our broken and self-destructive nature is reshaped so that the lamb will lie down with the lion; the pathological liar will love the purity of truth; the pedophile will associate with children without abuse or exploitation; the powerful and self-serving will find joy in serving others; and people who hide their pettiness in the cloak of good works will be free to live without being restricted by shriveled hearts.

But this takes time. We live in a world where we measure our lives in seconds, minutes, months, years and millennia. There is nothing wrong with impatience as we look ahead to that time of peace and joy. We're made that way. But creation is measured within different time patterns. The beginning of this cosmos (at least the one we know) happened long ago. From the discoveries of Einstein and others, we have learned that time is relative. If we could travel faster than light, it is estimated that time would slow down. All of this is to say that once we leap the boundaries of our space-time continuum, we have no idea what time will look like. Such hopes are not foolish dreaming. It's the very essence of Christian faith: God will bring those who love and serve him into that ultimate place of forever living.

God has created humans with the ability to make choices, regardless of how destructive they may be. Because we live in community, bad choices ripple into the worlds of others, for better or for worse. Also God allows pain to act as a warning that something is wrong. Only dead pain cells fail to awake us for our own protection. In emotional terms, it is when the cells of the heart are alive to what is good that they can detect what is wrong. Life is changed when we understand that living includes the happy and sad times and that suffering is part of the fabric woven by a good and loving God. Yancey comments:

> Is God speaking to us through our suffering? It is dangerous and perhaps even unscriptural to torture ourselves by looking for his message in a specific throb of pain, a specific instance of suffering. The message may simply be that we live in a world with fixed laws, like everyone else. But from the larger view, from the view of all history, yes, God speaks to us through suffering—or perhaps in spite of suffering. The symphony he is composing includes minor chords, dissonance, and tiresome fugal passages. But those of us who follow his conducting through early movement will, with renewed strength, someday burst into song.[33]

Seven

FINDING HAPPINESS (OR KNOWING HEALING WHEN I SEE IT)

If we believe health is to feel happy, we will be disappointed, for being healthy and feeling happy are not the same. Though feelings of happiness come to us as we walk the paths of hope and faith, they are too fleeting and unpredictable to be viewed as synonymous with health. At the high end of our concerns is how we feel. We seem driven to monitor our feelings, and from that we determine our wellbeing. The impulse to search our way out of hurt to a euphoric sense of feeling happy, can be dangerous however. Although I believe that having a relationship with God will lead to a deep sense of wellbeing, we'll get into trouble if our prime objective is to feel happiness. As British writer Malcolm Muggeridge wrote, "Happiness is like a young deer, fleet and beautiful. Hunt him, and he becomes a frantic quarry; after the kill, a piece of stinking flesh."[34]

Don't get me wrong. I too want to feel good. When I end a day feeling unhappy, I'm likely to chalk that day up as being less than worthwhile. But in times of sorrow, it's critical that we ask, "What do I mean by happiness?" Then, "To what degree is my feeling quotient important in this search for healing?"

There are times when I come across a book so rich in understanding that I want to recommend its reading. Such is the case with *In Search of Happiness*, by Dr. James Houston, an Oxford scholar and founder of Regent College in Vancouver, Canada. In his guide to personal contentment he warns us that,

Happiness does not fall into our lap by chance or accident. It is the fruit of a particular way of life that includes discipline, self-reflection, influence upon others, personal contentment, security and inner peace. So happiness is not just a fad, nor is it a god, although in our society it is often pursued as if it were one or the other. Nor is it a destination, but a journey still unfinished. Happiness is certainly not the absence of pain, or otherwise it would be confused with plea-sure—as is often the case in our culture. So what is happiness? Happiness is everything that gives wellbeing to one's self; harmony and assurance to others; depth and perspectives to the spiritual reali-ties around and above us.[35]

He distinguishes between feeling happy and happiness, the latter which he equates with wellbeing. We rob ourselves of the deep and important meaning of happiness when we take it to mean how we feel today. Each of us has some kind of personal thermometer, measuring our feelings. But because it is emotionally based, it's rela-tive. If ten is the very best on my scale of what it means to feel really happy and I'm undergoing chemotherapy for throat cancer, happi-ness may be measured by being able to have a drink. For an athlete, being able to outscore an opponent may be the prime measurement of feeling happy. The values we give to a particular experience vary according to what is most important to us at that moment.

KNOWING OUR GOALS

In our search for ways out of hurt into healing, it's helpful to imprint on our minds what the achievement of the goal will look like. In our desperate drive to find release from hurt, we must not crowd out a discriminating view of what the search should produce.

I had wondered which title would best suit this chapter: "Finding Happiness" or "Knowing Healing When I See It." Though experi-encing the feeling of happiness is important, our prime goal is to find healing, which leads to the question, What do I mean by healing? For a person in the life-struggles of a terminal disease, healing means to be rid of the disease. But is physical healing even a realistic hope? If one is hurting from the death of a close family member, what then is healing? Surely it's not the loved one's return. It is in this sense that I link happiness to healing.

DISCIPLINE FOR WELLBEING

As a student at the University of Toronto in the 1960s, I sensed an enormous preoccupation with freedom. In those heady days of rebellion, throwing away restraints symbolized what was thought of as freedom. Though this counterculture mood produced all sorts of bizarre sexual and social behavior, it also in part overturned educational standards. In the debate over what constituted true education, a group convinced the Ontario government and educational authorities to allow free expression in education.

Out of this came Rochdale College, located on Bloor Street on the north side of the U of T campus. There students began their own courses while living in residence. It was not long before the residence and its so-called education degenerated into a helter-skelter environment. Courses were laughable, travesties of higher education. Drugs were available. Free love abounded. In the end the police had to move in, and the building was confiscated. The breaking down of barriers for unbounded personal choice did not lead to educational progress or the enhancement of students. Rather, chaos ruled. Freedom was anything but. Without boundaries, education became a laugh. Lives and relationships were destroyed as our generation learned the hard way that health and wellbeing require discipline and focus. The notion of complete freedom was a destructive illusion.

JESUS DEFINES HAPPINESS

While the decade of the 1960s was driven by a secularization—pushing faith from public life—it, in turn, produced a revival of the spirit. Along with the craziness of my generation, there emerged on many campuses a remarkable interest in matters of faith. With their long hair, the Jesus People were often indistinguishable from their peers, but they were, in fact, a social movement fueled by the deep desire for freedom in a holistic way. Instead of breaking the guidelines of reasonable behavior, they avoided the lifestyle and drugs of the hippie culture and obeyed the teachings of Jesus, discovering that he had something tough to say about what it means to be blessed or happy.

Jesus' famous Sermon on the Mount begins with nine ways a person can come to happiness. His reference to *blessed* in Greek literally means *happy*. Being a Jew, Jesus thought and worked from a Hebrew mind set. The Hebrew word for *blessed* is *ashr*. The writer of the Proverbs says, "Blessed (*ashr*) is the man who finds wisdom . . . . Her ways are pleasant ways and her paths are peace." Here *ashr* means to find the right path. If you are confused and looking for the right road to take, when you find that right road, you are then "happy." Happiness in Jesus' terms means getting on the right path.[36]

Though it seems strange that one who is thirsty, poor or persecuted can be happy, in his sermon Jesus refuses to buy into the notion that being in a happy state is the same as having a worry-free or trouble-free life. His upside-down wisdom is hard to understand and even harder to accept. Yet we are made whole when we see how true his teachings really are (Matt. 5: 3–11).

Earl Palmer divides Jesus' nine-fold path to happiness into three groups.

1. The first part of the journey begins with the Hebrew *ashr*, or happiness, that comes from the inner, personal pathway of life. We often assume that our sense of wellbeing rises from right circumstances. We assume if only we had this or that, if only this person

would love us, if only our employer would recognize our gifts, if only we had anticipated the latest swing in the stock market, then our lives would be happy. If we assume that happiness is a function of what happens to us, what people do or say to us, or what societal issues affect our lives, then healing is a long way off.

Jesus understood this. Even though his Sermon on the Mount may be baffling, to understand his following criteria of happiness is to understand the essence of healing:

HAPPY ARE THE POOR IN SPIRIT; THAT IS, THOSE WHO KNOW THEY ARE POOR

The New International Version of the New Testament states, "Blessed are the poor in spirit for theirs is the kingdom of heaven." What a strange combination. What does poverty of spirit and inheriting God's best have in common? And how does that connect with healing and happiness? In *The Message,* Eugene Peterson puts it this way: "You're blessed when you're at the end of your rope. With less of you there is more of God and his rule." James Houston says, "When we come to the end of our own virtues and realize our inner poverty, it is then that we can start to experience 'the kingdom of heaven' in our lives."[37]

It's not poverty of spirit that brings new life. Rather, it is through knowing how low we are and how much we are in need of God's kingdom that the door to his resources is opened. Being poor in spirit and denying our need will get us nowhere. The turnaround is in being aware of our poverty, looking it in the face and opening ourselves up to the richness of God's wealth. When we know of our poverty we're moved to his abundance. Upon his appointment, Canadian Governor-General George Vanier wrote to a friend, "I feel it is only in weakness that I can glorify God."[38] In his poverty he had room to receive what would make him strong and what ultimately made him one of the great governors-general in Canadian history.

HAPPY ARE THOSE WHO MOURN, THOSE WHO FEEL DEEPLY THE SENSE OF LOSS AND THE PAIN THAT GOES WITH IT

If we think it a paradox for poverty to be a prelude to happiness, how can mourning bring about a happy heart? Eugene Peterson interprets Jesus' words this way: "You're blessed when you feel you've lost what is most dear to you. Only then can you be embraced by the One most dear to you."

When tragedy strikes, mourning is vital to recovery. A friend lost his child but seemed unable to grieve. Finally, with therapy he opened the door of his grieving, which enabled him to find release. Mourning is a gift from the Creator. Allow the hurt to rise in open grief so that feelings connected to loss have ample opportunity for expression. It's the strong who cry; the weak assume that being strong means we must bottle up hurt. Mourning allows the release of anger and inner stress. Then, as Peterson says, we can be embraced by the "One" we know is the ultimate source of healing. In mourning we lance superficiality from our lives and deepen our walk of faith by seeing others and their needs. From tearful eyes we see better.

How odd to say that when we are poor in spirit and when we mourn, we are on the path to healing and wellbeing. Jesus teaches us that to be on this journey brings blessedness, or happiness. Happiness has nothing to do with how we feel, but rather depends on our being on the right path.

HAPPY ARE THE MEEK OR THOSE WHO HAVE A SANE EVALUATION OF THEMSELVES

The word *meek* is often confused with *weak*. That's unfortunate, because meekness can be instructive for us as we search for healing and happiness. To be meek is to be sensitive to who we are. A prime characteristic of Moses was his meekness; that is, he learned to know who he was. That wasn't always true. Early in his life he killed an

Egyptian who was harassing a Hebrew, and he had to flee for his life. As a result he learned, over time, to understand himself. So when he was instructed by God to go before the Pharaoh and demand the release of the Hebrews, knowing his speech impediment, he asked that his brother Aaron speak for him. In short, Moses was meek in that he knew who he was.

Meekness is seeing ourselves in the proper perspective. When we hurt we can mistakenly believe that no one has experienced such pain, and we end up unduly magnifying our own struggle. Don't blow the circumstance out of proportion. Healing comes when we line up our grief with other realities. If I lose a child, it is then that my spouse needs me more than ever. Either parent can become so overwrought with their own hurt that they forget their partner, and the marriage can suffer or even break up. Lacking meekness is when we allow hurt to overpower us and cause our perspective to be lost. Happiness can be ours when we see our current situation on the broader landscape.

HAPPY ARE THOSE WHO HUNGER AND THIRST AFTER RIGHTEOUSNESS, THOSE WHO HAVE MOVED BEYOND THE VARIOUS FALSE OPTIONS OF THIS GENERATION AND HAVE DECIDED TO SEEK GOD'S TRUTH AND CHARACTER

Healing is my reward when I know the grander story of creation. The tragedy with materialism—which our educational system assumes is the only way to understand life and creation—is that it robs us from seeing human life on the wide cosmic tapestry. Along with a preoccupation with things material and the assumption that happiness is in the accumulation of gadgets, trips, retirement plans and property, we end up stunted in knowing what it means to be human. We are first made from beyond ourselves, and we will rest only when we find our lives in God.

Another tragedy is when some expressions of Christian faith rob us of the grandeur of God and reduce his nature to life-depleting liturgies, worn-out phrases, trite doctrines, restrictive legalisms and tired structures in boring meetings. God is greater, grander, more complex and fascinating than any other object of human search. Look for that which is magnificent. Celebrate the simple yet complex wonders of the cosmos. Drill to the deep regions of his culture-transforming truth. Rise above the petty and banal, and see the wider horizons of grace. We, finite and earth-bound, will not be so forever. We are part of what has forever been and what forever will be. Take hold of what is yours, what has been offered, and let it bring you healing and fill you with happiness, not that which is giddy or bouncy, but profound and weighty.

2. Palmer's second group of rules to follow on Jesus' path to happiness involves establishing loving relationships with others.

HAPPY ARE THE MERCIFUL, THOSE WHO REALLY LOVE PEOPLE, NOT IN A THEORETICAL SENSE, BUT IN A CONCRETE WAY

There is always the excuse that, for example, if you have a type-A personality, which is goal driven, people may not play as important a role in your life as they do for someone whose personality type leads him or her to focus on helping others. I'm not discounting the variance between personalities, but Jesus doesn't say, "For type-A personalities I'll make an exception." We are all called to find health by loving people.

The point here is that we can't wait to love others until we are healed and have reached the plateau of happiness. Healing happens as we love. There is no magical moment. Because love is an act of will, we need not look for the right feeling or emotion. We are to love now, and in the process we will discover that happiness is the byproduct.

HAPPY ARE THE PURE IN HEART, THOSE WHO HAVE SIMPLIFIED AND UNCLUTTERED THEIR AFFECTIONS, HAVING CHOSEN TO OBEY THE RIGHTEOUS WILL OF GOD

I interviewed a pedophile whose front-page story had caught the attention and anger of Canadians. He had done his time in prison; his wife left him; his life was shattered; and the two boys and a girl he molested were damaged for life. In prison, feeling bitter remorse for his actions, he came to personal faith and completed an undergraduate degree. Now out on probation, he wanted to complete graduate studies. I asked about his life. He told me about his childhood, in which he too had been sexually abused. He frankly described to me his struggle with thoughts of children.

"But how about today?" I probed.

"I guess it is like alcoholism: one always must be careful, knowing that it's a weakness."

"But with this inclination, what do you do about your thoughts?" I asked.

His response was direct: "When impure thoughts come, I immediately invite Christ to invade my mind and take those thoughts into subjection. It's an action I initiate, and I've found that by doing this my mind is cleared."

Happiness rising out of purity is not a natural human trait, even though it may be found in some. As this pedophile described, it is our responsibility by the exercise of our will to invite purity into our thoughts and give shape to our activities. We are constantly barraged by symbols, suggestions and blatant invitations to lower our standards. Film producers know that sex scenes will attract a larger audience. The human mind is inevitably drawn to the salacious. How happy is one whose mind is uncluttered, free from the baggage of impurity, free to respond to good impulses. That is health, and it comes as I feed on that which brings health.

Happy Are the Peacemakers; That is, Those Who Share the Health and Wholeness of Peace with the People around Them

Broken families need someone to bring peace. Nations need brokers to bring warring factions together. With the collapse of the Soviet Union and the cessation of super-power polarity, we hoped for world peace. Then conflicts escalated in Asia, Europe, Africa, Ireland and elsewhere around the world. In healing, look for opportunities to foster peace. Speak peace in conversations of labor and management. Overcome an inclination to point to the failures of others or expound on the mistakes of politicians. Find metaphors and examples that enhance goodness and draw people together. Happiness comes from initiating peace.

Nowhere is conflict and hurt felt more, it seems, than in the break up of a marriage. Often the two sides seem to be living on different planets. Descriptions of the same event have little in common, and hurt and bitterness are so deep that discussion becomes vitriolic, mutually destructive. Try to do the opposite of what you feel. As offended and violated as you are, what might be the effect if you were intentional about peacemaking? Healing and happiness would be the byproduct.

3. The third way to find happiness is tough and unrelenting.

Happy Are Those Who Are Persecuted Because of Righteousness

Happy Are Those Who are Persecuted on Christ's Account

These two promises don't seem to lead to happiness. But within the framework of Jesus' offering, they do. Jesus was aware that his call would arouse the anger of the ruling elite. Even as I write, I know of Christians in China, the Sudan, Iran and many other countries who are at risk when they witness to their faith. The same may be true for a Christian medical professional who refuses to participate in a hospital abortion. A young person refusing to join peers in taking drugs may feel rejection and outright hostility. And what does an executive do when the ethics of the company violate his or her Christian vision of truth and goodness? These people all pay a price—for some it's life itself, for others it's their reputation or livelihood.

Jesus understood that his claims cut sharply across the grain of culture. But he promised happiness and health for those who take the risk, uphold what is good and are willing to accept the consequences. Viktor Frankl, in recalling how he survived the Holcaust, wrote that happiness can come about through "one's personal dedication to a cause greater than oneself or as the byproduct of one's surrender to a person other than oneself."[39] Happiness surely does not depend on being persecuted. But Jesus does remind us it can derive from the most frightful of situations.

Eight

STEPS ON THE PATH OF HEALING

THE POSITIVE EFFECTS OF PAIN

Pain can dry out our souls, leaving us fatigued, worn and alone. We needn't succumb to defeat or disillusionment. Instead, our lives can be enriched and our vision renewed. The power of vision to lift us from the ashes of defeat finds its roots in the Apostle Paul's insight: "And we know that in all things God works for the good of those who love him . . ." (Rom. 8:28, NIV). Paul allows us to see that even in sorrow there is ultimate good.

Some wonder if there can be good in an evil act. Taken at face value it seems absurd. So where is it "that in all things God works for the good"? It is in how I respond to what happens. Circumstance can work in my life to the good. This is where my own will and commitment come into play. If my focus is only about my circumstance, it prevents me from seeing beyond to something good which may be at work. The Apostle had solid grounds for his claim. Writing to Christians living under the harsh treatment of Rome, he offered the encouraging promise that, "in all these things we are more than conquerors through him who loved us." For Paul nothing, including death and demons "will be able to separate us from the love of God that is in Christ Jesus our Lord" (Rom. 8:38, NIV).

But suffering is not the end of any story. Story after story tells us of people who go through the very worst of tragedies and allow their personal hurt to enrich rather than destroy. There are many positive effects pain can produce in our lives. These include:

I CAN COME TO TERMS WITH MY HUMANITY

It is easy to take life for granted, especially when it is moving along without mishap or hurt. Then, without warning, disaster strikes. A hurricane sweeps in from the Atlantic, washing over already-struggling countries of Central America, killing thousands. The normalcy of life is shattered, and the expectation that life will continue as it has been is no longer there. What then?

We are forced to see that life is fragile and temporary, be it from the sudden death of a loved one, a doctor's announcement of impending death or the unforeseen loss of a job. Do we continue to struggle on in our grief, oblivious to who we are as individuals? As harsh as it may seem, the dark vortex of pain gives us a moment like no other when we can begin the search to know what it means to be human.

I CAN REST WITH THE WOUNDED

It is sad but true that most of us tend to ignore others in pain. Hospitals are uncomfortable places for many, because we simply don't know what to say. Speaking with those in sorrow, I've asked, "What do you want people to say to you?" Most say, "Don't try to be nice or clever. Just be with me. Don't try to lift my heartache, because even though I know you mean well by it, I can see it's an enormous effort, and I then have to try to make you feel comfortable."

PAIN IS AN EQUALIZER

None of us gets through life without being hurt. Regardless of our place in society, no matter how successful others (or we) think we are, at some place and time pain will be our lot. It comes simply by living and sharing in the lives of others. We can't manage our lives to keep safe. Being financially well off, well educated, or well intentioned does not guarantee a trouble-free life. The Princess of Wales' broken marriage and her struggle with bulimia startled many because it was assumed that living in a palace was idyllic. But in that seeming paradise, she too hurt. And it was in knowing and seeing her hurt that we connected with her. When we experience pain we enter into the crucible of humanity where we are all trying to work out our faith and hopes.

When you're in that moment of sorrow, the empathy and understanding of another's tears brings solace and comfort. Through our own pain then, we understand the importance of emotional solidarity with others.

I CAN LOOK BEYOND POSSESSIONS AND PENSIONS

When I reached fifty, I suddenly realized we hadn't properly prepared for our later years. Saving and investment then became a priority, although a little late. What I didn't expect was that this became too high a priority. We can also tend to evaluate personal success by the status of our job, our standing in the community and our financial wellbeing. When grief hits, in that instant those priorities get shoved aside. Life and relationships loom large and critical. If we let it, grief can help us see what really matters, and by so doing, give us the impetus to arrange our lives so that life itself is at the core.

GOD BECOMES PERSONAL

The need to know what is beyond our own resources can turn our eyes beyond family and friends to see, maybe for the first time, the God who exists and cares. But more than that, we can see our need to invite his life to become ours. When we come to see our connection with the Creator and that his imprint is on us, we have an enormous opportunity to learn and to know God is not only for intellectuals, but for everyone. We can learn and discover insights about a life that we may never have thought was there. As Malcolm Muggeridge wrote, the most important things in life I've learned have come out of suffering.

Dietrich Bonhoeffer, the German pastor who was thrown into a concentration camp for resisting Hitler, testified in his final written words what God meant to him. Bonhoeffer was so despised by the Nazis that one of the last acts of Himmler—who directed the Nazi s s and coordinated the concentration camps—was to order his execution on April 9, 1945, just days before the Allies liberated the camp. In the first stanza of a poem "New Year 1945," Bonhoeffer wrote,

> With every power for good to stay and guide me,
> comforted and inspired beyond all fear,
> I'll live these days with you in thought beside me,
> and pass, with you, into the coming year.[40]

HEALING REQUIRES ACTION

Following a lower back injury, my first inclination was to protect it by not walking or jogging. Then one morning I realized how foolish that was. Pulling on my shorts, T-shirt and runners, I slowly walked out to the lane behind our summer home. I could feel the sharp pain from the sciatic nerve down my left leg and the stiffness across my lower back. How much easier it would have been to retire to the couch and believe that relaxing my muscles would bring healing. Not so. The path of healing requires painful steps. Not many years ago, patients would be hospitalized for days after an operation. Now we know better. The sooner a patient is up and moving, the faster the healing.

We can choose whether or not to move towards healing. Therapists have analyzed why some refuse to take those steps. They may not want to move on from anger or hurt out of a desire to punish. Others, reluctant to face change, choose to stay in the familiarity of their pain. Some relive their hurt, believing that by reliving it, life will change. Others are held back by the fear that moving forward will only make them vulnerable to being hurt again.

STEPS FOR THE JOURNEY

As we work our way along the path of healing there are important steps to take.

CHOOSE YOUR ATTITUDE

Viktor Frankl reminds us that, even in the most horrific of situations, one's attitude has an enormous role in shaping what happens: "The experiences of camp life show that man does have a choice of action. There were enough examples, often of a heroic nature, which proved that apathy could be overcome, irritability suppressed. Man can preserve a vestige of spiritual freedom, of independence of mind, even in such terrible conditions of psychic and physical stress . . . everything can be taken from man but one thing the last of human freedoms—to choose one's attitude in any given set of circumstances, to choose one's way."[41]

"In you lies the power to choose, to commit," writes Stephen Covey. "Commitment is the great bridge that connects vision to action." He continues, "If commitment is not there, actions will be governed by circumstances instead of vision."[42]

The kind of person you want to become is greatly influenced by your inner decisions, and not from outside influences alone. We can, even under adverse circumstances, decide what shall become of us.

CHOOSE TO LOVE YOUR LIFE

When asked by Jesus which was the great commandment, a lawyer replied, "To love the Lord God with all our heart, soul and mind and our neighbor as ourselves." "You're right," remarked Jesus.

And herein is a topic of some controversy: to love our neighbor as ourselves.

The love of self is not an act that is self-centered of selfish. The notion of a selfish love contradicts Jesus' great commandment with love as the defining reality. Jesus saw loving self as rudimentary to loving others. The loving of self allows us to know what it means to receive acceptance and care. This, along with a loving God, is the starting point of loving others. When we labor in sorrow, we are prone to direct our energies inward. A sign of healing is when we practice the great call of Christ and begin to love others.

Loving myself is to admit that my life matters. Love, by its essence, is to say to another, "Your life matters to me." When we come to see how important our lives are to God, we begin the walk away from the inner loneliness and crippling sadness that characterize those who have no Godly love of self.

When we look at ourselves with a selfish, self-serving spirit, we add to the crippling weight of our pain. Selfishness kills. It distorts our understanding of self, and we end up deceived, not empowered. On the other hand, our suffering may stem from failing to meet that primary call of the Creator to love what God has made. We are not enhanced when we put ourselves down, thinking that by so doing we lift others up. True love looks out for the best and is, above all, honest. Healing comes when we look at what God has made and, with thanks, celebrate his creation.

BECOME A LISTENER

The call came late at night. A friend had gone to her lawyer's office that day to sign divorce papers, and upon her return to her apartment, she discovered that her new partner, with whom she had taken up shortly after her marriage broke up, had moved out. She was heartbroken. Of all the days for this new friend to leave—on the day she formally ended a marriage of twenty-five years. It was almost too much.

I wondered what to say to her in this time of grief. I told her that, although she felt the pangs not only of the death of her marriage but now also of the new relationship, this was a great moment. For in her failed marriage she had learned some things about herself that were important to her growth. In taking up so soon with another person, the narcotic of this new relationship put to sleep those valuable lessons. Though this new friend's departure caused more pain than she thought she could bear, it took away the painkillers that were camouflaging her underlying source of pain. To change metaphors, the earplugs to her soul had been removed so that she could hear again, even if, at first, the noise was louder than she could stand.

Taylor Caldwell wrote a deeply moving book called *The Listener*. In it she described the tragic lives of people who visited a place of healing. No one said how the healing came about, and as one reads, your curiosity grows. Finally you learn. Each hurting person walks into a room and stands before a tapestry of incredible beauty. But nothing is said. In one's desire to meet God and find out answers to agonizing questions, there is nothing but silence. After waiting and waiting, each person succumbs to the need to speak of one's pain and, in so doing, comes to hear themself.

In dealing with lower back pain, I've come to listen to my body. When stress builds and I don't take remedial action to lessen the stress or release it by exercise, the pain intensifies. My body speaks, but when I fail to listen, it cranks up the decibels of pain until I have no option but to listen.

RELEASE YOUR EMOTIONS

In learning to understand our humanity, many of us in the West face the challenge of letting our emotions mature. People are rarely taught how to do this. Some of us learn through psychology courses, a self-help book or therapy.

Stephen Covey notes the dangers of this in warning us that unexpressed feelings never die. They are buried alive, and they come forth later in uglier ways: in over-reactive comments, in anger, in violent expressions, in psychosomatic illnesses, in ignoring people, in extreme statements or judgments or in other forms of acting out in dysfunctional and hurtful ways.[43]

Apart from the emotionally laden soap operas of our media-drenched society, crying is seen as a sign of weakness rather than as a gift. To allow our inner emotions to spill out is a way of defining our humanity. To hurt is human; to cry is to express that humanness. In the expression of grief we come to understand our very nature. To let our pain surface gives us more "data" about what's going on inside, about our true orientation to the situation. It lets us connect our thinking and feeling by giving us a more accurate basis for decision making. Indeed, some unexpected reactions occur in crisis, when buried emotions assert themselves.

Gerry Clemenger, who suffered the loss of her husband and daughter, said she could look back over those fourteen years and see how God unfolded her life. Then she clarified her perspective: "Life can be good, but it is never the same. But I have learned that eventually the tear bursts turn into recalling a treasured memory. You keep crying, but you remember the treasure."

Connecting with our own hurt lets us recognize it in others. During my own time of darkness, one day while having lunch with a colleague, I saw hurt in his eyes. After years of leading, recruiting and overseeing people, I had never seen it as I did that day. I had known when they hurt by what people said or did, but never had I seen it in their eyes. The reason I could see it that day was that I knew what it looked like in my own. Along with all the lessons I learned in those dark nights, one of the best was to see with different eyes.

LEARN THAT EMOTIONS NEED TAMING

In 1793 the French adopted "the goddess of Reason" in an attempt to overcome the forces of emotion and irrationality by trying to banish the notion of mystery and the transcendent from intellectual life. Such thinking assumed that society should stick to finding truth from the powers of rationality, science and logic. James Houston identifies three assumptions this brought: that happiness is self-motivated and not received through human relationships; that thinking is superior to feeling; and that the more intellectual a person is, the more superior he is.

In Houston's view, this ascendance of reason also rides roughshod over desire, when desire is viewed as the enemy of reason. "Desire opens us to many creative possibilities—especially to faith and the creativity of trust. When people are strong-willed and dominant, but seek to become gentler and more open to others, to begin to desire great things of God is often the only way that their hearts can change."[44] We can fall into the trap of believing that emotional pain is irrational and therefore invalid. But we are created to cry, be happy, enjoy and feel. Such is our inheritance.

At the same time, out-of-control emotions only limit our ability to sort out who we are so we can move onto the path of healing. In reaction to the dominance of reason, science and technology, some people rebel. Various types of New Age thinking go "to the opposite extreme by putting . . . faith in the most bizarre forms of magic and irrationality. Belief in ancient magic and the use of drugs are not responsible ways of responding to the cold rationalism of our age. We need instead to recover the fullness of our humanity, which has been neglected for so long in the modern world."[45]

Healing will be our reward as we accept this gift of feeling, recognizing that it complements thinking. Together they form the dual lanes of the highway of wellbeing.

WIDEN THE LANDSCAPE

When a friend dies, it becomes an opportunity to look past the immediate landscape and wonder what life is beyond the grave. I know some respond with, "Don't give me that business about the by and by. That's fantasy, and at the moment I only want to deal with reality." I understand. But life takes on a different hue if we can— for at least a moment—push back our cultural assumption that the only life we'll live is what we see: the physical. Think about what life might be like once we've completed our days on planet Earth. Why should we assume that in the great expanse of space and time, that the only life we'll ever live is from physical birth to physical death? Doesn't it seem plausible that the birth of an infant is only the beginning? Of all that I know about God's creation and of the coming of Jesus of Nazareth, I've come to believe that life goes on forever. The genius of a Christian view is that life is, as a friend once remarked, when we write our genetic code for eternity. The hope of a future with God is a powerful source of strength to those living in daily pain. Appreciating that life exists on a grand scale beyond death is not a romantic overlay to ease or rationalize our hurts. Without this wider view, we limit our possibilities.

We are taken up with ourselves from birth. As parents our task with children is to help them mature so they don't focus on themselves but include the interests and needs of others. But even as an adult, as much as I want to go beyond myself, at times it seems almost impossible to define what I do and who I am apart from those self-interests. The pain of life gives me opportunities to see in a new way that Jesus' maxim—"save their lives by losing them"—is the essence of life. Like the seed, we don't really die but are reborn to multiply in ways never before imagined.

Mother Teresa brought a new definition to the meaning of "a good life" by giving her life to the poorest of the poor in an era driven by a materialistic binge in which fiscal moguls, screen stars and over-paid sport jocks were chosen as heroes. Within this frenzy of bowing before human shrines, she redefined what it means to be truly human.

SEE BEYOND THE CIRCUMSTANCES

When I am overcome by hurt, it is difficult to see anything but my circumstance. Healing, however, comes as I see that all of life is not defined by my situation. Hurt's deafening roar, though warning me, is more than a signal that something is wrong. It is also a signal that I need to get outside of my limiting moment and see it in a wider context. Recall the problems of Job, who in his paralyzing sorrow, was asked by God:

Where were you when I laid the earth's foundations? . . .
Who decided the dimensions of it, do you know? . . .
Who laid its cornerstone when all the stars of the morning were singing with joy? . . .
Who pent up the sea behind closed doors when it leapt tumultuous out of the womb? . . .
Have you ever in your life given orders to the morning or sent the dawn to its post? . . .
Have you an inkling of the extent of the earth? (Job 38:4–18, *The Jerusalem Bible*).

This is tough. God pushes Job to see that, though his pain is significant, in the overall scheme of things, there are elements of life that are larger than self. God is awesome. His presence overshadows all of life. The incredible galaxies that come from his creative work still bow to his command. If, in times of relative wellbeing, we build into our thinking this larger sense of life, then when we enter into pain, we have a reservoir from which we can draw. In that sense establishing times for personal prayer and devotion become the building blocks for healing.

This "seeing beyond" does not come easily or with an easily read devotional guide. It builds and develops through months of taking time to hear and see. It comes by the discipline of allowing our hearts and minds (feelings and thoughts) to learn of God's capacity in creation and his love for you, the creation. Of course, we want the quick fix. We want the toxic elements cleared from our system this very day. This cannot be done when we are dealing with either physical or emotional pain. A body left to sedentary living will scream in exhaustion when forced to run the length of the airport to catch a plane. I can't push my body to do what it hasn't been developed to do in everyday living. And neither can we expect that of our emotions. If life is consumed with watching sports or soap operas, we can't expect to find a storehouse of insight and understanding filled and ready for access.

There are two initiatives we can take today. First, obtain a devotional guide to help focus the mind. Second, reserve a place and time for fifteen minutes each day to allow your inner life to begin to focus on something other than hurt. The key is to realize that life is not only as you now see it. The blinding hurt distorts vision and builds walls that seem impenetrable.

LEARN TO PRAY

The sounds of praying are the moans and groans of the soul. Most of our prayers are learned as children. For those raised in more liturgical churches, prayers are fixed. Others learn prayers that at first seem spontaneous but over time become largely based on memory.

When we hurt, we are most honest. To pray in anger, if that is your mood, is okay. Too often we assume God is nervously rubbing sweaty palms, shifting from one foot to another, anxious that we might ask questions too big for him to handle. Go ahead. God is God. Let your feelings give way to words. Allow the noise in your soul to reach his ears. And since he already knows, your telling won't be a surprise.

My brother David recalls the long, tough nights in the early months after Jill died:

> During the first few weeks, everyone commented on how strong we were. Then the real stuff of grief set in. Any resolve that we were going to nobly use this event to help us minister to others was soundly thrashed by the rounds of grief that seized us. Grief, that virus of the soul, had a course when triggered. It would start with a flutter in the pit of the stomach and then finally satisfied, would leave us fatigued and lonely.

For the first few nights, we mixed spasms of grief with attempts to sleep. A sensation would take shape when I'd close my eyes: a dark evil in the form of an amorphous black cloud would seem to enter the room with hands extended, seeking to grasp us around our throats. The first time it occurred, we tried to pray it away, to no avail. I have no idea what started us to vocally praise the Lord for the wonderful life that we had been given with Jill. But as soon as we did, the cloud would leave the room, and we would fall asleep. We knew of the Scripture verse that told us God lived in the praises of his people, so we should not have been surprised by what happened. However, theology is not the elixir or potion whereby grief is fixed, but rather as we experienced, it is the quiet Presence of the Christ who weeps with us, who accompanies us in the valley that brings God near.

CHOOSE TO SEE LIFE ON AN UPWARD PLANE OF GROWTH

Philip Yancey points out that God bothers with us because his concern is that we grow, just as parents assist their children from childhood to adulthood. His illustration is of a father who, in his love for his child, carries her so she won't stumble and ends up preventing her from learning to walk. His desire to protect leads to disability. The father needs to let the child stumble and fall, and by so doing she will move up the incline of personal growth and learning.

In *The Gulag Archipelago*, Alexander Solzhenitsyn wrote, "It was only when I lay there on rotting straw that I sensed within myself the first stirrings of good. Gradually, it was disclosed to me that the line separating good and evil passes not through states, nor between classes, nor between political parties either—but right through every human heart. . . . I nourished my soul there, and I say without hesitation: Bless you, prison, for having been in my life."[46]

GIVE IT TIME

Most of us live life in a hurry. The pace of our globalized world creates an internal assumption that any problem must be solved now.

Our grieving hearts and hurting minds are like a broken bone, need-ing time to mend. If we work with our grieving, we learn the value of patience. Indeed, we must allow ourselves the gift of time. If we try to short-circuit our grieving process, we are likely to feel the surge of a new crisis and then wonder why the blowout. Sometimes practicing patience means ignoring someone who pushes us too quickly to get on with life. Respect for time, together with other acquired values, allows us to live in more healthy ways as we allow the crisis to pass.

TAKE RESPONSIBILITY

Instead of traveling the path to wholeness, some choose to slump at the side of the road, convinced there's no point in making an effort because they are at the mercy of other forces, victims of life. This non-action may seem less painful, but living as a victim will only suck you further into the morass of self-pity and disability.

Sometimes the unfairness of life throws us badly off course. If we had assumed that good people doing good things are guaranteed good times, it comes as a shock to discover that neither life nor God hands out frequent-flyer points for those who are worthy. On the other hand, it seems quite unfair that some people waltz through life missing its potholes and avoiding its traffic jams.

Treating ourselves as victims shuts down the process of healing. If you have suffered because of someone else's action, you are a victim, through no fault of your own. Yet healing for you still includes resist-ing the inclination to continue to blame all of life's wounds on others.

Who among us doesn't have regrets? Although there are hurts that come through no fault of our own, much of our sorrow comes from failures resulting from our own choices, actions we've taken or not taken. To face that and admit our complicity, is part of our healing. As difficult as it may be, to refuse to bow to denial or defensiveness is to feel the healing process at work. The tendency of the human personality to pretend that strength is in denial—so that our role is either minimized or eliminated—leads to further hurt, moving us in the opposite direction from healing.

UNDERSTAND THAT CHOICES HAVE CONSEQUENCES

Along with taking responsibility for our actions, we need to accept responsibility for their consequences. An acquaintance faced this when, having recently made a confession of faith, he learned he had lung cancer. He was upset with God because he had assumed that, as God had begun a work of spiritual reconstruction on him, he would also cure this man from years of smoking. Though his past was forgiven and "cast into the sea of [God's] forgetfulness," to find healing he had to accept his own responsibility for what he had done to his body.

A good question to ask is, "Why did God structure life this way?" He could have created life so that suffering would be impossible. If so, we would be in that world now with no pain, knowing only grace and peace. So why didn't he? I don't know. But I do know that at the heart of his earthly creation is the freedom to make choices. So in that sense we can't have it both ways: the freedom to choose and no hurt resulting from our choices. Freedom gives us space in which we make choices, but with that comes consequences.

Sadly, many of our poor choices hurt others. We see it in the devastated faces of the parents of a reckless teen driver, of children shunted from one parent to another after a family breakup, of employees out of work because of business mismanagement.

For King David of Israel, choosing a night of indulgence led to a broken home, fragmented relationships and deaths. He had seemed to "have it all." He began caring for sheep and ended up ruling a Middle East kingdom. His leadership was nothing short of spectacular: he united his country, and people loved him, trusted his wisdom and admired his courage.

But that wasn't enough. One spring evening from his upper garden, he saw a beautiful woman, Bathsheba, bathing on a nearby roof. Caught up in sexual passion, he arranged for her to be brought to his palace. A few weeks later, she sent back a message: "I'm pregnant."

In an attempt to cover up, David told his general to send Bathsheba's husband Uriah home from the battlefront. When Uriah arrived David told him to go home and be with his wife, but Uriah refused, saying, "My lord's men are camped in the open fields. How could I go to my house to eat and drink and lie with my wife? As surely as you live, I will not do such a thing."

Still determined, David got Uriah drunk. Even so, Uriah stayed with his men. David became desperate. He instructed his general to "put Uriah in the front line where the fighting is fiercest. Then withdraw from him, so he will be struck down and die." When David received news of Uriah's death, he said casually to the messenger, "Don't let this upset you; the sword devours one as well as another." Then he married Bathsheba, assuming the matter was fixed and over.

Weeks later the prophet Nathan arrived at the palace and told David of a rich man who, instead of using one of his own sheep to feed a guest, stole a poor man's pet lamb and "prepared it for the one who had come to him."

David was furious. "As surely as the Lord lives, the man who did this deserves to die!"

Nathan looked at his king and said, "You are the man! This is what the Lord, the God of Israel says: I anointed you king over Israel and I delivered you from the hand of Saul. I gave your master's house to you, and your master's wives into your arms. I gave you the house of Israel and Judah. And if all this had been too little, I would have given you even more. Why did you despise the word of the Lord by doing what is evil in his eyes? You struck down Uriah the Hittite with the sword and took his wife to be your own. . . . Now, therefore, the sword will never depart from your house, because you despised me and took the wife of Uriah the Hittite to be your own."

David acknowledged his sin and God forgave him, but David still had to face consequences (2 Sam. 12:13–14). Then began the heartache of this great king, minstrel, war hero and diplomat, the one the Scripture describes as "a man after God's own heart" (1 Sam. 13:14). First, David and Bathsheba's son died at birth. Then the havoc David unsheathed reached others in the family. Amnon, one of David's sons, raped David's daughter Tamar. Absalom, a favorite child, took revenge and ordered his men to kill Amnon. Then David lost Absalom, when he fled from his father in fear to live for three years in exile. Eventually David relented, letting Absalom return to Jerusalem on the condition he stay away from the palace. But this too failed. Absalom built up a small army, and David was forced to flee. Finally, in a battle between the two forces, Absalom was killed.

In the sad but liberating soliloquy of Psalm 51, David returned to the source of life:

> Have mercy on me, O God,
>   according to your unfailing love;
> according to your great compassion
>   blot out my transgressions.
> Wash away all my iniquity
>   and cleanse me from my sin.
>
> For I know my transgressions,
>   and my sin is always before me.
> Against you, you only, have I sinned
>   and done what is evil in your sight . . .
>
> Create in me a pure heart, O God,
>   and renew a steadfast spirit within me.

David knew something deeper was required.

You do not delight in sacrifice, or I would bring it;
  you do not take pleasure in burnt offerings.
The sacrifices of God are a broken spirit;
  a broken and contrite heart,
O God, you will not despise.

David's remorse and his return to his original principles did not undo what had been done. His son died. His family continued to feel the ripple effect of David's failure. But he moved ahead.

The beginning of resolution in broken homes and relationships is to see that our failings begin, not with what happened in the process of fragmentation but in our broken connection with the Creator. For it is in this relationship that we can work out our human relationships.

ADMIT THERE IS NO RETURN TO EDEN

Augustine, a leader of the fourth-century Church, ran from God for some thirty years. He finally confessed, "Our hearts are made for you, O God, and they will not rest until they rest in you. . . . Too late, too late, O Lord, have I loved you. . . . The ability to remember is indeed a sad privilege."[47]

Wasted years are painful. Sometimes I awake in the night, recalling my shortcomings. For example, I'll remember a statement I made in public that may be unfair, misleading or simply foolish. I'll break out in a cold sweat and wish for all the world I could recall those words. But I can't. The way is not back, but ahead.

The Bible doesn't give much attention to where human suffering comes from. Instead it pushes us forward to ask about the purpose and value of suffering. That flies in the face of Western thinking, in which we assume that personal happiness is an inalienable right, and when we suffer we demand the reasons it occurred. But in the Scriptures, the way is always forward. In knowing that life on earth moves into the City of God, we must try to stop going back to relive or figure out the past. Lost days, missed opportunities, misplaced investment of time, outright wrongdoing—all are part of our history, but the longing to go back and redo it is fruitless. God is not interested in remaking the past. Our call is to make the past right by moving forward on the path of obedience. As we do, God affects our lives and brings about a reconstruction, preparing us not only for a lifetime but for an eternity. Healing is apparent when we move past the compulsive need to know the whys of the past and try to right the wrongs. Except for doing what I can to address those wrongs by soliciting forgiveness and making restitution, the way is forward.

In spite of his sins, King David understood this. When Bathsheba's child was born and lay ill, David remained in seclusion. When he finally learned that the child had died, he got up, put on fresh clothes and ate. His courtiers were confused and asked, "Why are you acting this way? While the child was alive, you fasted and wept, but now that the child is dead, you get up and eat."

He answered, "While the child was still alive, I fasted and wept. I thought, Who knows? The Lord may be gracious to me and let the child live. But now that he is dead, why should I fast? Can I bring him back again? I will go to him, but he will not return to me."

In his classic *City of God*, Augustine bears out the immense importance of continuing on the pilgrimage of faith. Healing is not found in the purity and simplicity of Eden. We received truth and wisdom, not from the tree of good and evil, but from the rugged tree that graced the hill of Golgotha on the outskirts of Jerusalem. To return to Eden is to try to undo what is part of the past so that wisdom from today's pain can be worked into our earlier years. This is not only impossible, but a waste of time. The path of healing leads us to accept what we have done in life after Eden and directs us to find a new life that grows continually out of the tree of Calvary.

Life is a pilgrimage. For those who trust in Christ, it is but a pause in eternity, a sojourn calling us to move on. One of my colleagues encourages us when we struggle with errors by saying, "Let's move on." There is something life-giving in that. Although we don't want to ignore the need to address our failures and correct our flaws, healing is evident when we travel forward.

As we move on, we give God the freedom to reconstruct our lives. Recall that after the deaths of her husband and daughter, there came a time when Gerry Clemenger prayed, "Lord, I open my hand. I accept your will. I don't like it, I don't understand it, but I accept it."

PURSUE NEW OPPORTUNITIES FOR WELLBEING

Some years back, while struggling with depression and a sense of failure, I took Hebrews 12 as my daily fare. Time after time I would turn to read its promise. First the writer tells us;

> My dear child, don't shrug off God's discipline,
>   but don't be crushed by it either.
> It's the child he loves that he disciplines;
>   the child he embraces, he also corrects.

The writer continues with the reminder,

> Strengthen your feeble arms and weak knees. "Make level paths for your feet," so that the lame may not be disabled, but rather healed (Heb. 12:12–13, NIV).

The warning is to be careful so our weak and hurt legs won't be pushed to take on more than they are able. While wounded we are advised to avoid taking rough paths that exacerbate our woundedness. Instead, we should search out easier paths until our legs are sufficiently healed. Or to put it another way, be kind to yourself when you hurt. Give yourself time to be healed.

When your legs are strong, then do as the writer of Hebrews advises. In *The Message* Eugene Peterson puts it this way, "So don't sit around on your hands! No more dragging your feet! Clear the path for long-distance runners so no one will trip and fall, so no one will step in a hole and sprain an ankle. Help each other out. And run for it!"

New opportunities come as we knock on doors. If we don't knock, they won't open. Whatever we do, we do with the knowledge that God is alongside, guiding, coaching and empowering. But he has given us both the freedom and the responsibility to make choices. Where we end up is not because of some master blueprint in heaven. Although God knows the beginning to the end, that is not the same as saying it has all been worked out and all we have to do is get up in the morning.

Jesus said, "Ask and it will be given to you; seek and you will find; knock and the door will be opened to you. For everyone who asks receives; he who seeks finds; and to him who knocks, the door will be opened. Which of you fathers, if your son asks for a fish, will give him a snake instead? Or if he asks for an egg, will give him a scorpion? If you then, though you are evil, know how to give good gifts to your children, how much more will your Father in heaven give the Holy Spirit to those who ask him!" (Luke 11, NIV).

As painful as the walk toward healing is, the only way it will come is when we begin the process. At first it will be slow and painful. Yet to begin the walk will lead to opportunities that, in our darkest moments, we never imagined possible.

When my brother David decided to do what he had always wanted to do—to help the poor of the world—he sold his business and became part of Opportunities International, a worldwide team that provides small loans to the poor in developing countries so that they can start their own businesses and build financial stability for their families. It was out of his mind-numbing personal hurt that he found the opportunity to help those who were economically crippled. This door opened at a time when life was dark and the idea of finding new open doors seemed remote. The lesson is to refuse to allow pain to keep you from the pursuit of doing good.

FORGIVE

The other side of asking God to forgive us is to do the same for others. Some refuse to forgive because they think they're letting the person who wronged them off the hook. Instead, they want to punish that person with their own anger. In the end this backfires, and we remain shackled to memory and hurt.

Reaksa, the Cambodian boy who survived the killing fields, learned this through long years of pain:

> One of the most difficult lessons of my life has been to forgive those who killed my family. To forgive is a very unpleasant thing to do. It seems unjust to forgive those who killed my family. They were evil people and they should be punished.
>
> Years of rage, hatred and hurt began to affect my health, and most of the time I felt sick and depressed. A few years after I became a Christian, I realized that I had to find a way to cut the root of anger and bitterness from my heart. If I refused to forgive those who killed my family, I would be forever living an unhealthy life. I would never gain internal peace. I must forgive so that I can get rid of the emotional baggage that has been holding me back; so that I can be free to do and be whatever I decide instead of stumbling along according to the script written by a painful past....
>
> It has taken me many years to learn to forgive, and I am still learning. For years I tried to forget the traumatic images that bothered my life. I tried and tried, but without success. In fact, the more I tried to forget, the more images I captured.
>
> I finally became aware that forgetting is not the way to learn to forgive. No one in the world is able to forget a tragic loss of someone in his or her family. Nothing will turn back the clock and remove the unpleasant and painful events from my life. It is not fair that my family was killed without reason; nothing will ever change the injustice of that. Forgiveness does not work that way.
>
> As I wrestled with it, I realized that forgiveness begins with remembering and accepting the corrupt nature of human beings. In particular, I have to work through and accept the painful experiences of my past. It is like swallowing the rage, anger and hatred that has been blocked in my throat for years. These experiences of pain have

been teaching me a great lesson of life, both about not becoming victimized again and not victimizing others.

Making a decision to live after a major loss is not easy; it requires putting my willpower and power of thinking ahead of some very powerful emotions. I realize that I cannot wait until I feel better and decide to live again. If I wait until I feel better then I will miss out on a genuine ingredient of life that God wants to show me. I will miss the significance of forgiveness. I must make a decision to forgive those who killed my family. Since God has forgiven me, it is right for me to forgive those who killed my family, even though it is painful to do so.

A few years ago I was invited to share my story at a conference. In a question period after I finished, a young girl asked me, "Reaksa, if you were to meet one of the evil [soldiers] again, what would you say to him?" It was the first time anyone had confronted me about forgiveness. I summoned up courage from my heart and made a decision to publicly commit to what I had been struggling with and learning in private.

"If I were to meet one of them, or all of them again," I said, "I would tell them that I forgive them for what they have done to me and my family."

When I made the decision to forgive, it was a matter of letting the hatred go from my mind. I no longer wish for the [soldiers] to suffer . . . . Since I have forgiven those who killed my family, my life has been changing. The rage, hatred and negative emotions have been uprooted from my soul by the power of the Holy Spirit. I have more peace of mind. I am not saying that I have forgotten the bitterness in my life, but the emotions are not choking my throat any more.

Forgiveness is a special gift from God that I have discovered in my life. Forgiveness has nothing to do with forgetting; it is love's revolution against life's unfairness. Forgiveness is the spiritual power that breaks the prison that the memory of the killers creates in my soul. It washes away the bitterness. Forgiving is the process of healing the soul.[48]

ADOPT NEW VALUES

When Pekka Varvas, the man who had suffered the business failures, was asked what helped him through his second round of business problems, he described how family support and new values made a difference.

Two things: First my relationship with the Lord. Even though I was at times confused, I knew I had to focus on eternal issues. Second, it was my incredibly supportive wife. Through it all Anita stood by me. I eventually concluded that if I worked as a security guard—no matter what I did—I would still have my wife and kids. I would still be needed and loved.

There was a time, though, when I didn't understand why the second business failure happened. This time I was honoring the Lord. The steps weren't out of arrogance. I thought about it, prayed about it, my wife prayed about it, and together we decided. Still I failed.

But I've come to see that it's not success or failure that is most important. Instead it's how I deal with them. God is with us through both success and failure. Life is measured by relationships. We will experience success and failure in life. God is concerned with how we deal with our relationships in the midst of both. How we cope with failure is a test.

Then I asked, "How has your life changed by what others would call a failure?"

I try to discipline myself to spend more time with the Lord, in private and in church. I've also changed my perspective. Previously I was involved in big projects, boards. Now I prefer to have relationships with a few or a small group, with those who touch each other.

Also you can't let money control you. You have to control money. That hasn't been an easy lesson for me to learn. I've sacrificed a lot of things I shouldn't have for the sake of making money. I'm a little sadder now but a whole lot wiser. Success and failure are things God uses to do what is important for me.

Use My Wounds to Heal Others

John Cambridge, an editor for *Hansard* (the official record of parliamentary proceedings) at the Ontario legislature, had no idea he would be let go. On a Tuesday morning, his director called him into his office and said, "It has nothing to do with your performance, but we have to let you go."

John went to the human resources office for a few minutes to hear about his entitlement, then cleaned out his desk while a security guard stood nearby to make sure he did not access his computer. "In half an hour you're out the door."

"For the next few days I felt numb," John remembers. "Immediately afterwards I had a coffee at a sandwich shop. Then I felt incredibly angry. I wondered how my wife would react. She manages a major law library and is used to handling crises. But the first thing she said was, 'Don't worry, we'll sort out something.'" Because she also handled human resources, she said, "You shouldn't be so surprised. That's the way it's done everywhere. What you went through is classic textbook firing." It was also a classic hurt.

"But I have a hard time being convinced [that way is] best for the person," John continues. "What is most damaged is one's feeling of self worth, no matter how much someone says, 'it's not your performance.' If I'm so good, why me? I wondered at first.

"After I got over the initial shock, I felt God wanted me to take a change of direction. That's what sustained me. The normal reaction in such unpleasantness would be to blame someone or strike out, perhaps because of feeling victimized. So having the attitude that God guided me negated that bitterness."

I asked John, "What have you learned about trusting Christ?"

He replied, "I certainly learned that though things may be difficult, God hasn't abandoned us, nor has the situation happened because of something we did. Yet after two years, I can't say I know why God let it happen."

Even before he was let go, John was involved in Out of the Cold, a program that helps the homeless and others in need from October to the end of April. Once a week his downtown church provides a hot dinner:

It began with ten guests and by the spring it had seventy-five. People walked miles because they heard the food was so good. As servers we bring food to our guests and sit with our own meal and chat and listen. Two of us sit at each table with six guests. I marvel at the astounding variety of personalities, some well educated.

After I was let go from my job I felt a real affinity with our guests. Many are on welfare, disability or have physical problems. Like me they are trying to maintain a home. A lot have gone through what I did but will not be able to come through as I have. But it's not their fault.

If I sit down now with them, I can say I know how it feels to be fired. I can be sincere. Our experience was the same, the circumstances the same. God and I could use my experience. Honestly I don't feel there was any time I blamed God.

It wasn't work. It was a social evening. I got to the point where I resented it if I had to miss the Tuesday dinners. I no longer saw the guests as a group but as persons. For a few weeks before Christmas we sang carols around the piano, but our guests didn't stop with the holidays, and quite a few kept on singing hymns each week. At the last dinner in April an Asian lady who lives in a couple of rooms gripped my hand and thanked us for providing the time. Doing something positive was probably one of the things that helped me. Turning attention from oneself and getting a perspective is therapeutic.

There are times we may have to accept that our hurt and suffering say nothing. However, that shouldn't keep us from turning them to an advantage. Out of our of sorrow we are called to do good, and out of our failure we can inspire others.

Nine

THE POWER OF WOUNDS

The front door burst open one Saturday morning and a five-year-old ran in, crying as if her little heart would break. Her father, working around the house, heard the cry. He knew it was more than the cry of a child with a skinned knee. It came from deep inside. He picked her up, holding her and stroking her back in an effort to calm her.

"What's wrong? What has happened?"

When the sobs sufficiently subsided, the girl asked, "Daddy, what's a bastard?"

Her father understood instantly. While playing with neighborhood children that morning, his daughter had learned that she was adopted and perhaps even that her birth parents weren't married when she was born. His heart sank. Although his adopted daughter didn't know what the word meant, she knew it was unkind.

He was stunned. In his arms was the little one he and his wife had come to love every bit as much as the older child born to them. He had never really thought about the difference of their births. Both were their children. The very word *bastard* angered him. But now was not the time to resolve his feelings. She needed an answer, an answer of truth and love, not from a dictionary.

He sat on a kitchen chair, rocking her in his arms. What could he say? he wondered. Then it came to him. Turning the tear-stained face toward him, he said, "Sweetie, you remember the story of Jesus? Well, his mommy's name was Mary, and he was born before she was married. The reason was that it was God who made Mary pregnant with Jesus. But when Jesus was your age, his friends didn't understand that. They only knew what their parents had gossiped about Jesus.

"*Bastard* is a harsh word. But it simply means that your mother got pregnant before she was married. So you and Jesus have a lot in common. He too knew what it felt like to be made fun of. He also felt the hurt when his friends were unkind. Jesus understands."

As the father recounted this special moment, he remembered his daughter turning to him and asking, "Daddy, is it true that Jesus knows how much it hurts when friends are so mean?"

In that life-changing moment, the child learned what it takes many of us a lifetime to learn: Jesus heals our hurts from his own wounds.

Let me introduce you to Jesus the healer of pain. No person can reach into your inner caves of hurt, dark with foreboding and fear, and light a lantern of truth. Only the Creator, who knows us beyond our knowing, can right the wrong and restore the broken heart.

Out of the Hebrew Old Testament came a promise written around 587 B.C. The prophet Micah looked down the highway of time and saw Bethlehem, an inconspicuous village with a population of some 200, as the site of the birthplace of the Messiah. In our sentimentalized approach to Christmas, we romanticize his birthplace even though his birth was anything but romantic. Having traveled from the north, Mary laid her newborn in a cow's feeding box. From this small village and with an obscure parentage and a pregnancy outside of the ordinary, Jesus began his life on earth. He lived as a vulnerable infant in need of the constant care of his mother. This was God, Jesus the Son of God. The Creator of all life had to be human, with all that implied. From the moment of his birth until he left the earth, Jesus engaged in the human dilemma.

In the unremarkable village of Nazareth, he was raised in a carpenter's home. His family life was disciplined: "He learned obedience from what he suffered" (Heb. 5:8, NIV). Under the unrelenting power of Rome, he lived with his family and worked with his father, all the time learning the tough lessons of life from what he experienced.

From here his public work began, lasting until he was relatively old at the age of thirty. His brief three years of teaching and healing ended on a Roman cross reserved for political agitators, thieves and murderers. But precisely because he walked the road of truth and hurt, Jesus offers to us a faith rooted in his own pilgrimage and life. The Old Testament prophet Isaiah looked forward to this day of the Messiah and said, "By his wounds we are healed" (Isa. 53:5). Jesus knew why he had come. Without wavering from his appointed task, he took the road from Galilee, the place of his childhood, south to Jerusalem, the city of Roman power and religious authority. His life and message, though popular with common folk of the Middle East, threatened the power brokers. They would have none of it. Yes, Jesus could have stayed in the security of the north, but his calling was to expunge evil and give humanity the means to be healed.

THE WOUNDS OF DEATH

At the heart of Christian faith is the death and resurrection of Jesus and no moment in the Christian calendar is as important as the celebration of the Lord's Supper. The form will vary depending on the Christian community, but it is a time we are called on to remember the crucifixion and death of Jesus. At the last meal he took wine—symbolizing the blood he was about to shed—and a loaf of bread—symbolizing his broken body nailed to a rough-hewn cross—and asked his disciples to continue to celebrate his death until his return.

Nothing so profoundly describes Jesus as the powerful symbols of wine, bread and the Roman cross. While we now craft crosses as works of art or jewelry, during Jesus' time the cross was the most painful and repulsive symbol. It had nothing to do with beauty, but rather fear, repression and cruelty. It was a public display of the way the ruling army dominated and suppressed the people of the country of occupation. A few years before Jesus' birth, Jews who had tried to overthrow the Roman army were hanged by the hundreds on crosses along roads leading to and from Jerusalem. Stripped naked, these men died slowly. But even death didn't bring dignity. Their bodies were left rotting on the crosses while scavengers ate their flesh. It was Rome's way of wielding a harsh and humiliating club against those they feared.

This too was the death of Jesus. A contemporary comparison would be the infamous death necklace of South Africa's days of apartheid turmoil. A car tire would be dropped around the victim, trapping his arms, rendering him helpless. Gasoline would then be poured into the tire and ignited, leaving the victim to burn to death. We wouldn't create costume jewelry symbolizing a burning tire today any more than they would have used a cross for decoration in Jesus' time. It spoke of agonizing death.

Jesus' wounds were real. This was no Greek legend. In the struggle for good, the God-Human Jesus of Nazareth felt each penetrating thorn driven down in the cruel crown devised by his tormentors. As the cat o' nine tails lacerated his back, his pain was no less than that felt by the toughest criminal. The physical exertion of dragging his own cross outside the walls of the city so exhausted him that the soldiers had to call an onlooker into service. As the cross dropped into the hole on the hill of Golgotha, the nails ripped through his hands and feet. Wounds. Blood. Pain. Unimaginable pain.

My first observation with overwhelming grief was as a boy. A woman and her daughter had driven from Star City to Saskatoon to meet the woman's husband and son. When they arrived they learned that the men had just been killed in a car accident. The two women sat at our kitchen table in shock and grief, living through the early hours of trauma. I had never heard such weeping and despair. I recall sitting on our bedroom stairs listening to their wailing while Mom and Dad, with gentle tones and loving words, sought to bring some measure of solace. The experience was awful. A dark and hopeless gloom descended over our home. Their sorrow was so deep because the loss was permanent. The father and brother would never return. Nothing could be done except to find a way to go on living. I felt selfish, but knowing there was nothing I could do, I wished they would go away and leave us from having to live in their sorrow.

We avoid the cross because it is ugly. At a recent art showing at the school where I serve as president, a young, talented artist painted a picture called the *Holocaust of Abortion*. This very large canvas hung on a wall leading to our chapel. Within hours there was strong objection from some students repulsed by the ugliness of fetuses lying in a heap. Yes, it was ugly and repulsive, but should we avoid the truth because it's objectionable?

One reason I find the cross disturbing is that it speaks to me of injustice. Jesus got no justice whatsoever. As I look up at his hurt and death, I am driven to notice injustice elsewhere. The picture of Jesus dying on a Roman cross is a relentless reminder of acts of injustice repeated day after day. As I write I hear the news of further "ethnic cleansing" in Serbian-held territory. Then a young man known to be gay is pistol-whipped and left to die on a Wyoming range. We'd rather hear good news. We feel as if we can't take such extreme injustice any longer because it calls us to do something. And that is a bother. We're already overrun with duties and personal needs.

As I look at the cross, I turn away because of my sense of power-lessness. What in the world can I do? I wonder as I imagine the Roman guards surrounding the three crosses. In the face of the power brokers of life, we don't have the solution and even if we did, we'd have no means by which to initiate it. So we think.

Too easily we paint cute and false pictures of this Jesus. Out of our various cultures, Jesus emerges as whatever we need him to be. Some paint Jesus as a kind of Santa Claus, jolly and happy, wanting to bring all the good boys and girls what they deserve. Others turn to

Scrooge as a paradigm of Jesus as a tight-fisted old man who rains on our parades. I've noticed that some see Jesus as a celestial bellboy, serving our every whim. In some Marxist rhetoric, Jesus is portrayed as a revolutionary guerrilla, forever upsetting the status quo. On the opposite side is the image of Jesus as the ultimate CEO, successful and always the winner. The pictures are many and most often false.

DRAWING HEALING FROM HIS WOUNDS

So we redraw the cross to avoid the reality of Jesus' hurt. Yet it is only if we see it for what it is that we can enter into his death and draw from it our healing. The cross of Jesus speaks to us in many ways. First, it tells us that we are worthy. We may be criminals or outcasts or feel a huge guilt due to our personal failures, but as we envision Jesus' death, he looks at us as he looked at those standing on the hill near his cross and reminds us that we are the reason for his coming.

The cross also tells us that we are forgiven. As much as our own rebellion and self-centeredness contributed to his death, we know he lifts our guilt and declares us forgiven. Guilt is debilitating. It not only reminds us of what we've done, but it continues to affirm how despicable we are. We are good actors, pretending our failures never happened, and if someone points an accusing finger, we raise our eyebrows in mock surprise, "Not me!" Yet in our hearts we know it is true. And Jesus knows. There is nothing about who we are or what we've done that escapes his notice. With all of that information at hand, he looks down and tells us we're forgiven. The reason for the suffering and the resulting wounds is now lifted. We are free to walk into eternity knowing our failures will no longer be held against us.

In being forgiven we are also being healed. Our wounds, be they old or recent, come by way of someone violating God's laws. They may come because of our own misadventure or without our complicity whatsoever. Regardless, they are wounds that need healing. The bleeding wounds of Jesus are the source of our healing. Not only does he feel our wounds, but we can see in his wounds the giving of life by the Creator. So reach back over the span of time and by faith invite Jesus, the suffering Creator and Healer, to clean your wounds, to apply his medicine and protect them so they can heal.

The cross is also a reminder that we are chosen, called upon to be part of his beloved. Yes, he died for the whole world. But this does not imply that we have nothing to say about it, that it just is, or that we are not part of his kingdom. The fact is that as wide is his mercy is, he calls on us to say yes or no. To be invited to share in the world of this Creator-Healer is beyond my wildest expectations. But that is the invitation. We must choose to accept it.

The paradox of the wounded healer is that the cross, rather than speaking of bondage, sends out a message of freedom. As much as this notion grates against the ego of so-called Western enlightenment, the payment of our debts took place that day on the cross. By his death Jesus took our place, leaving us free to go, unhindered by the weight of our past. As much as darkness works to overload us with the weight of failure and unsettled accounts, Jesus snaps the chains that tie us to the failures of our past.

My brother David recalls:

One particularly dark moment, the valley of grief happened around what might be called a crisis of faith. It was not rooted in some theoretical dialectic. It was hatched in the inconsistency of our profound pain and the Scripture where I understood Jesus to have said, "Come to me, all you that are weary and are carrying heavy burdens and I will give you rest. Take my yoke upon you, and learn of me; for I am gentle and humble in hearts, and you will find rest for your souls. For my yoke is easy, and my burden is light." When relief was not forthcoming in our appeal to him, I concluded that I had lost my relationship with Christ. In fact, I may never have been his follower, for surely he, reported to be a God of love, would not have abandoned me at that point. This was a serious problem, and I could not bring myself to speak with anyone about it.

I finally called a friend who is a psychiatrist, Dr. Irvin Callender, who agreed to meet with us weekly. I had read an article which claimed that 75 percent of parents who lose children to death, lose their marriages as well. That risk was too high to chance.

One day Dr. Callender offered me this insight to my anxiety of losing faith. "David," he asked, "recall the time Jesus was struggling under the weight of the cross as he was forced to carry it from the place of judgment in Jerusalem to the hill of Golgotha? He stumbled under the weight. He couldn't carry it alone. They had to recruit someone to carry the cross to the hill for him."

As he shared that with us, not only did the import of what he had to say reach us, but also that the Heavenly Father used a friend to speak to me specifically when I could not even express the additional pain from that sense of being abandoned by God.

As horrible and repulsive as the cross is, it speaks to me that Jesus has spanned the distance from God and creator to human life. The shape of the cross not only reaches horizontally to bring all of creation into its vortex, it also bridges the vertical space from above down to earth. Stretching across the gulf of separation, it connects human life with the divine. Jesus did that by his death. When he cried, "It's finished!" he implied that the work he had come to do was now complete. No longer was there separation between the created and the Creator.

In the Temple in Jerusalem, there was a thick curtain separating the worshipping Jews from an area known as the Holy of Holies. Once a year the high priest would go into this most sacred of Jewish places and sacrifice for the sins of the people. No one else was allowed to enter. However, when Jesus cried "It is finished," we are told that curtain ripped from top to bottom, telling all that no longer was it required that a person go through a temple priest to have his sins forgiven. That life now flows freely from God to man.

As we see the cross in its brutality, its rugged features inform us that the victory of Jesus empowers us in life. No longer victims, we rise from that hill of crucifixion empowered by Christ. The Roman soldier in charge of overseeing the crucifixions, bowed and admitted, "Yes, this must be the Son of God." He saw where the real power lay even when Jesus was ridiculed by a thief on an adjoining cross and appeared powerless. With all that Rome could do with its armies and laws, it was nothing in comparison to the divine power of whom some called the Son of Man.

We stand then as worthy, forgiven, healed, chosen and set free, now able to love, renewed with divine life and empowered to live Christ's life because we are loved. What he brings flows from an unfathomable love to us as his creation. He has a double interest in us. Not only are we his by creation but also because of what he has done to give us life. We are his in this second sense: we have been redeemed, meaning our debts have been paid.

To receive Jesus' healing touch, we uncover our inner eyes so we can see his wounds, realizing that he knows our hurts through his own, and so he feels our searing sorrow. It is toward Jesus that we walk on the road of healing. We understand that the overwhelming sorrow of our lives in no way eclipses his.

The path of healing opens onto faith as we come to see that Jesus is not a phantom or a ruse of historical illusions. He is real. He lived, died and rose again in a world that is ours, too. Not on Mars or on an interplanetary vehicle, but in this world. My faith rests on a reality proven again and again by history. Out of the Scriptures, we come to see Jesus' nature, message and power. So we can take the risk. We can walk past the point of no return. Are we apprehensive? Yes. But we know that the risk is not a leap into the dark, but rather placing our lives in the hands of the great physician. As writer Francis Schaeffer put it, Jesus is there, and he is not silent. His healing reaches inside, transforming us from brokenness to wholeness.

Yes, it's important that we seek out healing from friends and counselors. It's vital that we work at our feelings, right wrongs and restore those human elements we so need. Turning to the Healer is not to deny or ignore what we can do ourselves or what others can do to help us. Not one of us is an island. We need each other and we stand in strength when we recognize the great importance of community. But there is available the physician who not only as Creator understands the most complex of emotions, but as one among us, he knows the agony of hurt and "is touched by the feelings of our infirmities" (Isa. 53:4).

Ten

WALKING THE PATH
OF HEALING

I live in a northern climate, where the seasons are distinct. As summer ends, the temperature cools, leaves turn brilliant reds, oranges and yellows, and shortened days tell me the winter snow will soon blanket the memories of summer. There is a certain sadness to losing summer; the short, cold days of winter speak of sleep. Then as winter passes, spring is announced as days lengthen, the sun moves higher, rays of sunlight strengthen, snow melts into rivulets and birds gone south return as we await the exciting rebirth of the earth.

The cycle of life requires death. As winter sets in, the trees' life-giving sap stops flowing. It appears as if death has come, but it is sleep. So it is with our lives. We live through the cycles of death and rebirth. Dreams die only to be reborn. Plans fall apart and are reconfigured beyond our original plans. We lose a job and on rebound may find one more suitable and satisfying. As we walk this three-fold path of healing we discover new elements that become intrinsic to our new-found lives.

DESIRE FOR MEANING

Most of us experience a desire to discover new things in life. This is a vital part of life. Without newness or change, we get stuck in the winter of our souls. An inner drive calls the seed to break free from its binding, daring to defy death, bursting upward to find sunshine and life and experience the birth of a new plant.

In your moment of "death" recognize that desires point to what can be. Appetite has good reason. The desire for family matches the human capacity to reproduce. God didn't give us inner desires only to keep us hanging. Thirst is to be quenched. Hunger is to be fed. Fatigue is to have rest. Life is like that. We are made to find what is authentic and meaningful, satisfying our deepest needs.

We also know that longing for the mystical is different from thirst, hunger and fatigue. Though we all gravitate to toys and pleasure, there are times we stare up at the stars and feel a deep hunger to know beyond creation to the Creator. Standing alongside the coffin of a friend, I want to know where he is now and what it's like. Holding our grandson, I wonder at the origin of his inner self, that person who will live forever. In short, I yearn to go behind the stage to the producer, behind the painting to the painter, behind the music to the composer.

When hurt and pain are present, my desire to know is accentuated. It's then I learn to welcome the hurt, as disconcerting and painful as it may be, for it points ahead. C.S. Lewis in *The Pilgrim's Regress* calls us to see beyond the false and superficial: "In the first place, though the sense of want is acute and even painful, yet the mere wanting is felt to be somehow a delight. This hunger is better than any other wealth. In the second place, there is a peculiar mystery about the object of this desire. Every one of these supposed objects for the desire is inadequate to it. It appears to me therefore that if a man diligently followed this desire, pursuing the false objects until their falsity appeared and then resolutely abandoning them, he must come out at last into the clear knowledge that the human soul was made to enjoy some object that is never fully given—nay, cannot even be imagined as given—in our present mode of subjective and spatio-temporal experience."[49]

"There is an empty room within the throne room of our hearts that only God can fill. In many cases this invisible emptiness inside us takes visible form."[50] James Houston echoes Pascal's famous line that within each of us exists a God-shaped vacuum. Yet some try to convince us that longings are only functions of microscopic elements that determine what we feel and want. In this scenario we end up as materialistic bits of life unable to know either the origin or meaning of life. If there is no design, there is no designer. But we know better. Human history tells us so. My experience of family convinces me of that. And the deep, long nights of the soul point me in the direction of discovery. To find Pascal's God-shaped vacuum and to understand Jesus takes more than rubbing salve on our wounds. It goes beyond the lifting of debilitating pain. We must probe deeper than a surgeon's knife. It calls for change.

BEING BORN FROM ABOVE

Jesus' promise of inner change was radical and startling news to the Palestinian community. Tapping into the Hebrew notion of the God-Human drama, Jesus takes it further by promising that life as we know it need not continue. Be it by circumstances or human propensity, we are not boxed in, fatally driven to repeat the sins of the past. We can be born from above. The proclivity to hate can be turned like a caterpillar into a butterfly.

It was John the Baptist, Jesus' cousin, who announced the arrival of Jesus on the Palestinian scene. John first appeared in the wild, preaching a baptism of life change and forgiveness of sins. People flocked to him from Judea and Jerusalem, confessing their sins, their life change symbolized by baptism in the Jordan River (Mark 1:4–5). John first introduced the need for personal change, which was later affirmed and taught by Jesus. Baptism in water became a metaphor for inner change, an idea from the Greek word *metanoia,* meaning a change of mind or change in one's outlook or thinking.

A Jewish scholar, afraid of what his colleagues might say, came to Jesus by night and posed a question: "Rabbi, we all know you're a teacher straight from God. No one could do all the God-pointing, God-revealing acts you do if God weren't in on it."

Jesus said, "You're absolutely right. Take it from me: Unless a person is born from above, it's not possible to see what I'm pointing to—to God's kingdom."

Nicodemus the theologian was baffled by this remarkable conversation. He asked, "How can anyone be born who has already been born and grown up? You can't re-enter your mother's womb and be born again. What are you saying with this 'born-from-above' talk?" It was too much for Nicodemus. It didn't fit his framework. He couldn't imagine what Jesus was talking about—something as illogical as climbing back into his mother's womb. So Jesus tried again:

> Unless a person submits to this original creation—the "wind hovering over the water" creation, the invisible moving the visible, a baptism into a new life—it's not possible to enter God's kingdom. When you look at a baby, it's just that: a body you can look at and touch. But the person who takes shape within is formed by something you can't see and touch—the Spirit—and becomes a living spirit.
>
> So don't be so surprised when I tell you that you have to be "born from above"—out of this world, so to speak. You know well enough how the wind blows this way and that. You hear it rustling through the trees, but you have no idea where it comes from or where it's headed next. That's the way it is with everyone "born from above" by the wind of God, the Spirit of God (John 3, NIV)

Like John, his cousin Jesus affirmed that we aren't doomed to walk our current path. We can change. In fact change is critical to the opening of the door of life to receive God's gift.

The inner change comes as Christ defeats what's been defeating us. Inner rebirth brings divine energy to help us face tragedy and sorrow with a new empowerment. *Metanoia* comes as God enters our lives. Jesus put it this way to Nicodemus: "This is how much God loved the world: He gave his Son, his one and only Son. And this is why: so that no one need be destroyed; by believing in him, anyone can have a whole and lasting life. God didn't go to all the trouble of sending his Son merely to point an accusing finger, telling the world how bad it was. He came to help, to put the world right again. Anyone who trusts in him is acquitted; anyone who refuse to trust him has long since been under the death sentence without knowing it. And why? Because of that person's failure to believe in the one-of-a-kind Son of God when introduced to him" (John 3:16–18, NIV).

With this good news, one would think we'd all go running to Jesus, embracing his offer. Unfortunately, that's not how it works. For example, even though there is good news informing us how to live healthy lives, we still cram our bodies with junk food and shun exercise. Just as we turn our backs on living healthy lives, so we turn away from the Creator and the offer of change. Why is that? Jesus throws light on that as he concludes his conversation with Nicodemus: "This is the crisis we're in: God-light streamed into the world, but men and women everywhere ran for the darkness. They went for the darkness because they were not really interested in pleasing God. Everyone who makes a practice of doing evil, addicted to denial and illusion, hates God-light and won't come near it, fearing a painful exposure. But anyone working and living in truth and reality welcomes God-light so the work can be seen for the God-work it is" (John 3:19–21, NIV).

Some years ago I co-authored with my medical-scientist brother Dr. Cal Stiller a book called *Lifegifts*, about the remarkable medical breakthrough of transplanting organs. In writing it, I developed an interest in this discovery, and we'd often talk about the interplay between body and spirit. One day I asked Cal about his understanding of Jesus' use of the metaphor of new birth. What he said has given me new insight into a vital part of what Jesus has to offer by way of inner transformation:

> I'm fascinated by the scientific parallel of the immune system to Jesus' promise to Nicodemus that he could be born anew. As a scientist, I see Jesus' use of the "born again" metaphor rising right out of what we have been discovering in the science of immunology.

You see, while the child is still in the mother's uterus, the immune system develops a sense of "self"—that is, what it will accept or reject. What the immune system "sees" prior to birth becomes what it sees for life. This understanding of self governs the immune surveillance system and is responsible for maintaining what we call the integrity of self. After the child is born, anything that the immune system then sees as being foreign, or not self, it rejects. If the body didn't have this kind of protection system and didn't have that immediate reflex to reject anything foreign, then enemies such as bacteria, viruses or fungi could invade and take over. The immune system is really the army on alert, protecting us from any invasion of disease. However, it needs to know what the enemy is and what it is not.

"Yes," I said, "I can see that the body builds a system to ward off any foreign invader, but how does this defense system change? For Jesus told Nicodemus he needed to be changed."

"That's where an understanding of what we are doing in changing the immune system fits into Jesus' message," Cal replied. "When we wanted to introduce to the body something foreign, such as an organ transplant, the immune system would see the transplant as not being self, or as an enemy, and reject it. It was recognized that the only way we could introduce another organ was to get the immune system to see that organ as self and accept it. So we found a way to reeducate the immune system. It is called "recapitulating ontogeny," which literally means 'to be born again.'"

I recalled Dr. Christian Barnard doing heart transplants in South Africa in the 1970s. The problem wasn't his surgery; he was a first-class surgeon. It was rather that the recipient body would see the new heart as not being self and in a few days reject the new heart, and both the heart and patient would die. So I asked my brother, "How did you reeducate the immune system?"

"We began to learn that we had to orient the body to accept the organ transplant and not see it as an enemy," he replied. "Through much research we learned that if we could take the immune system—as if it were developing in the mother's uterus—and expose it to something new, the immune system would reform in such a way as to see the foreign substance as self and not reject it.

"How can you can demonstrate that?" I inquired.

In two ways. First, we can open the uterus of a mother rat and inject into her white pup some cells from a black rat. When the pup is born, we can graft skin from the black rat onto the white rat, and it will accept that skin graft as though it was self. The reason is that, even though the skin graft from the black rat is foreign to the white rat, the immune system of the white rat sees the graft as being self.

Second, there is a biological phenomenon in the immune system called "neo-natal tolerance." Following the birth of a child, there is a window of a few months in which the newborn is susceptible to foreign influences. If, for example, the infant during this time takes on substances for which he did not develop a tolerance prior to birth, that foreign substance can distort the immune system's sense of self and the child will become tolerant to things he otherwise would have rejected. Since the child doesn't begin to make antibodies for a couple of months, the antibodies of the mother, present in the colostrum [the substance that mammary glands secrete just before producing milk] are essential in protecting the child. The mother's milk gives to the child's immune system its identity, or self, so that over its lifetime it knows what to fight off and what to accept.

"We do know that we are born with a 'fallen' nature, that is, we are prone as humans to act against God and live for ourselves. How is that changed?" I asked Cal.

Well, the new birth that Jesus promises is a parallel in my view to recapitulating ontogeny. Given that we are born, as you say, with a fallen human nature, the self is tolerant to things which, for example, are selfish. Spiritual concepts are rejected because they are foreign to what our spiritual immune system regards as self. So when Jesus told the Hebrew scholar Nicodemus he had to be born again, Jesus wasn't being frivolous. I think he showed his profound understanding of how both the physical and spiritual immune systems develop. He told Nicodemus he had to be born from God and remade so that his spiritual self would recognize and accept what up to that time was foreign to him. Without that rebirth (or recapitulating ontogeny), Nicodemus wouldn't be able to detect the difference between the new self and the old self. His system would be contaminated, and his spiritual integrity couldn't be maintained.

I said, "It's interesting that the Apostle Paul saw this when he said, 'Therefore, if any one is in Christ, he is a new creation; the old has gone, the new has come!' (2 Cor. 5:17, NIV). Then by his Spirit, Christ redirects our spiritual immune system to begin to accept what we in our fallen nature have rejected?"

"That's right," Cal responded. "If the immune system is not redirected or reborn, it continues to see truth as untruth, and good as bad. As in the case of a heart transplant, by reeducating the immune system, the body accepts the new heart as if it were self. So as we walk with Christ, our spiritual immune system is reborn so our self will see, for example, selfishness as foreign and reject it. I've wondered how people like Mother Teresa can love the sick and dying. It finally dawned on me. That's what Christ does for us by the new birth. He caused her spiritual immune system to be reborn so she can love what God loves and hate what God hates. She has a new sense of self."

"You said that the sense of self also develops after birth," I continued. "How would that link up with what Peter says in reference to people who have been born again? He says, 'Like newborn babies, crave pure spiritual milk, so that by it you may grow up in your salvation' (1 Pet. 2:2, NIV)."

Cal said, "This is only evidence of the ingenious insight of Jesus in telling us about the wonders of his recreating our interior lives. During the early months, because the child is susceptible to disease, it needs to develop a neo-natal tolerance. As the infant needs the antibodies of the mother to assist in the development of self, so it works when we are introduced to the world of spiritual life."

"That's why it's vital in the early days of one's walk with Christ to be nurtured by the antibodies of Christ's truth so that our system will build a sense of what is good and true and be able to distinguish that from what is harmful for our own health," I said.

"I agree," my brother replied. "Christ makes such sense in using this metaphor of being born again or born from above, as it brings about a recapitulating ontogeny in which our spiritual life is made alive to the laws of God. It makes so much sense."

It also made sense to a German prisoner, Jürgen Moltmann, who was held as a POW during World War II. While living in a cold cell with poor food, his greatest struggle was knowing of his country's failings and coming defeat. He carried with him the poems of Goethe and the writings of Nietzsche, but it was during his imprisonment that he began to read the New Testament and, as a result, turned to faith in Christ. He wrote, "I saw how other men collapsed inwardly, how they gave up all hope, sickening for the lack of it, some of them dying. The same thing almost happened to me. What kept me from it was a rebirth to new life thanks to a hope for which there is no evidence at all."[51]

Moltmann was kept alive by the rebirth which Jesus promised two thousand years earlier. His immune system had experienced recapitulating ontogeny—he had been born anew.

WHAT IS THIS NEW LIFE?

This healing journey along the path of hope, faith and love winds its way to a "new Eden." This is not reconstructing the past. Our past forever is and will exist as lived. We make no attempt to whitewash it or reconfigure it with memory adjustments or denial. Rather, we move to a new place in which we are called to be citizens, having a part in a new order, a new way of life. This new life includes:

A GIFT FROM GOD
Metanoia, or being born again from above, comes from the very

heart of God. This new life develops a riverbed in which the tireless stream of God's love flows. It's life that has been poured into people throughout the ages. It's a story told again and again in lives changed, born from above.

One such story is that of Johnny Lee Clary, former grand dragon of the Ku Klux Klan in Oklahoma. Raised by a father who hated Afro-Americans, he was taught at an early age to shout racial slurs. His mother sent him to Sunday school until one day his father heard him singing,

> Jesus loves the little children.
> All the children of the world;
> Red and yellow, black and white,
> they are precious in his sight.

That was as far as he got. "Don't ever let me catch you singing words like that again," his father thundered. And that was the last time Johnny went to Sunday school.

At eleven years of age, he watched his father put a gun to his head and pull the trigger. Johnny, in his subsequent hurt and loneliness, joined the Klan and at the age of twenty was made grand dragon of his region. One day he was asked to speak on radio on behalf of the Klan. Upon his arrival he was surprised to learn that the station had set up a debate with the Reverend Wade Watts, a leader in the National Association for the Advancement of Colored People (NAACP), an organization working to prevent discrimination against American blacks.

When Johnny refused to shake hands, Watts said, "Johnny, before we go in, I just want you to know that I love you, and Jesus loves you." After a bitter debate, Johnny ran into Watts outside the radio station, holding a baby in his arms. Watts asked, "You say you hate all black people, Mr. Clary. Just tell me how can you hate this child?"

Haunted by the question, Johnny continued building the Klan, moving higher in the organization. Whenever the question put to him by Watts pushed its way into his mind, he'd discount it and work all the harder. That is, until one day he brought together various groups, from skinheads to neo-Nazis, to organize them. Instead, they fought among themselves. Finally Johnny saw their hatred spreading out against each other. Johnny writes, "Suddenly I was repulsed by the poison that swirled around me. I felt sick to my stomach. I turned in disgust and walked out the door. . . . My life was a wreck. As the weeks passed, filled by a shame and worthlessness, I fell into deep depression—and the stultifying numbness of alcohol. Then came the terrible day I found myself in my shabby apartment raising a loaded gun to my head. Daddy, I'm following in your footsteps. There's no other way to go."

Sickened by this expression of hatred and hurting from the sense of rejection by a self-destructive father, Johnny knew there was something beyond the poisonous hatred of the Klan. Yet he had no one to provide a better model or offer a word of hope. Suicide seemed for him, too, the only way out of his hopeless despair. On the table he noticed an old and dusty Bible, like the one he had seen Reverend Watts carrying at the radio station debate and one like his grandmother used to read him. Putting down the gun, he picked up the Bible and found his way to the story of the prodigal son. In tears, he stumbled his way to faith. He joined a church, and some time later he called the Reverend Watts. The warm response was "Hello, Johnny Lee."

Johnny told Watts the story of what had happened in his life. After he finished the pastor said, "I've never stopped praying for you! Would you do me the honor of speaking at my church?" Some weeks later, as Johnny describes,

> When I stepped to the podium at this church and looked out over the congregation of mostly black faces, I told my story simply, not

hiding from the past or sugarcoating the depth and bitterness of my involvement. Then I told them how God had changed all the hate in my heart to love. There was silence when I finished. A teenage girl got to her feet and ran down the aisle toward me, arms open. I started to move in front of the altar, to pray with her. As I passed the reverend, I realized he was weeping. "Don't you know who that is Johnny Lee?" he asked quietly. "That's Tia. That's my baby." Yes, what I needed was a real family. And there had been one waiting to open its arms to me all along.[52]

A life focused on pain and self, needs the gift of life from the heart of God the Creator.

A LIFELINE

Lily and I worked various jobs during my last year of university so we could hostel our way through Europe that summer. One Sunday after lunch at a pension near Genoa, Italy, we walked out to the beach on the Mediterranean. It was lined with swimmers. Suddenly the relaxed, fun-seeking attitude of the beach loungers changed as we realized that a swimmer was being pulled out to sea by the undertow. People who knew the ways of the currents moved into action. Two men strained at the oars of a boat, slowly working their way across the bay to the swimmer. We could see the stress on the drowning man's face as he tried to keep above water. Treading against the power of the sea seemed to be more than he could manage. Time after time he slipped beneath an incoming wave. Just as we thought he wouldn't surface again, up he'd come, only to go through the cycle again: tread water, go under, rise to the surface, tread water. . . .

It was like seeing a film in slow motion. Though lasting only minutes, it seemed to go on and on. The swimmer gave it his best while the oarsmen fought on, knowing they were in a battle against time. When it seemed the swimmer was going down for the last time, an oarsman stood up and flung a life buoy to him. The swimmer grabbed hold, slipped it over his head and slumped in exhaustion.

Your hurt and struggle have gone on so long and drained you of energy and hope. Just when it seems you can't go any further, God's love is as a life buoy, holding you up above the outbound tide. The shore, which seemed an eternity away, is now within your reach.

A GIFT OF RECEIVING FORGIVENESS

As obvious as forgiveness is, we mistake its central role in healing. We tend to limit our forgiveness to those who have hurt us, rather than accepting forgiveness for our own part in contributing to our pain.

It was the night before Jesus died. At supper Peter, the loud disciple who seemed to open his mouth just long enough to change feet, protested that he'd follow Jesus anywhere. The disciples could feel the mood in the streets. They knew that the soldiers and the political and religious leaders were up to something.

Peter said, "Hey, Jesus, you can count on me. I'll stick with you no matter what." Jesus turned to him and said, "Thanks, Peter. However, I know that before sunrise tomorrow morning, three times you'll deny you even know me." After supper, they went out. Soon the Roman soldiers arrested Jesus.

Later when Peter was huddled around a fire, a young lady looked at him and said, "Hey, you. Aren't you one of those guys who works with Jesus, this rabbi from up in the Galilee?" Peter blushed and then in his blustery way said, "Get off it. I have nothing to do with him."

Twice more that night Peter told someone he didn't know Jesus. Then the rooster crowed. Peter looked up. It hit him. He had done exactly what Jesus said he would do: exactly the opposite of what he had promised he would not do. The historian said, "He went out and wept bitterly."

We all know what it's like to feel so low and miserable that you want to drop out of sight. The anguish over doing what you didn't want to do or what you thought you'd never do is so profound you wonder if you'll ever be able to look at yourself in the mirror again, let alone face the person you've wronged.

What did Jesus do? Three days later, while Peter was cooking fish on the shore, Jesus walked up to him. He didn't say, "Well, here you are, you big talker. Where were you during the very time I needed you to stand with me, when I was alone against the Roman army?" Instead he asked Peter a simple question: "Peter, do you love me?" He was forgiven. Gone was Peter's guilt and humiliation, never to be remembered (John 21). The Hebrew Scriptures use the metaphor "lost in the sea of God's forgetfulness" (Micah 7: 19). Someday you'll dredge up a past sin, and ask God for forgiveness. You can almost see the perplexed look on his face: "What's that? No, I don't recall it." You see it's gone, lost forever. When God forgives, he forgets. That's included in his gift of new life.

A GIFT TO BE ACCEPTED

I was raised in a minister's home. Very early on I came to understand the simple message of Christ. Throughout my childhood I enjoyed stories from the Bible. I memorized special verses and liked going to our small churches in the Canadian prairie towns and cities where I grew up.

But when as a high-school student I heard preacher Bernice Gerard in a public gathering tell us of our individual need of faith, it finally connected. The faith of my parents was not enough. The good things I was learning in church—as important as they were—couldn't give me what I needed. As a teenager looking forward to life, I woke up to the story of Nicodemus. I recall that Sunday night I told my buddy Lorne Ashton it was time I made my choice. I was going to invite Jesus of Nazareth to do what he promised, to give me birth in new life.

Since that October night in 1956 in Saskatoon, not once have I doubted this life from above, though I still struggle with life issues. It's made all the difference.

PAYMENT OF A DEBT

New life comes at a cost. Within the economy of creation, sin generates debt. Our original parents, when they ignored the imposed restrictions in the Garden of Eden, set in motion a force called sin. An encompassing human reality, sin is more than the total sins we commit. It is human rebellion. From the call of Abraham to begin the Hebrew race right down to the coming of Jesus, there has been an understanding that the debt of our sin needs to be addressed. And Jesus addressed it through paying the price by his death. My guilt was taken away as Jesus faced and defeated the powers of darkness, making good to God the Creator the payment for my sins and those of everyone who ever has or ever will live.

That payment is available for us to access. It is there for us to claim. As we do, the debt ledger of our lives are offset by Christ's payment, and we're declared no longer in debt. We're not free because the one to whom we owe the debt has dismissed it, but rather because it's been paid in full.

A SPRING OF WATER

I was raised in a church community that loved camp meetings. Our summer camp was located on the shore of Lake Manitou, a salt-water lake, saltier than the Dead Sea. What was especially intriguing was that it was called Living Waters Camp. Who in the world would call a camp located on a salt-water lake Living Waters? Those who had tasted of new life. On the edge of this so-called dead lake in Saskatchewan, pioneers saw instead the springs of life, even in the dry season of the "dirty thirties." During the nightmare of the Depression and in the dust bowl of the North American prairies, my spiritual ancestors thought in terms so freeing that even a salt-water lake reminded them of new life.

On the way to our summer cottage in Ontario, there is a spring running way down into a ditch. As we pass this spring, we often see cars lined up alongside the road. Most are cottagers living on the edge of a fresh-water lake. Yet they stop, get out of their cars and walk down into the ditch with their empty jugs to access a flowing spring. How much better if that spring were in my backyard. The gospel does just that: the spring of ongoing water is mine.

A New Way of Seeing

The word *orientation* describes the perspective people adopt to live their lives. We speak of someone's sexual orientation, a religious or secular orientation, or of a vegetarian orientation. A great deal of our original orientation comes from our upbringing and the influences of our culture. New life brings a new orientation. The three-fold path to healing begins with hope—we begin to see through something other than windows of hurt and pain. We orient our lives to see life in a different way. In that sense, we are oriented to a new way of seeing.

I'm not talking about a personality change, although for some that comes too. Rather, it is about an inner life connected to Christ. He said, "Be as I am." "Well, I can't," is my response. "He is God and human life come together, while I'm only human. So how in the world can I think as he does?" A new orientation means that this new inner life, over time, helps me see through different eyes.

A young man, out of his desperate need for inner change, made a confession of faith in Christ. Some weeks later he said, "Brian, I know something has happened."

"So how do you know?" I asked.

He explained that for years he had struggled with an overpowering sexual desire. His lifestyle had been permissive; he seemed driven by the need for sexual conquest. Following his turning to faith, something changed. First, his driving lust abated. As he told me, "I began to see women not as opportunities for conquest or as a means to a good time, but as real people to respect." His way of seeing others (in this case women) was reoriented from the inside out. That's the promise of this gift.

GRACE—RECEIVING GOOD THAT I DON'T DESERVE

These next two aspects of a new life in Christ are like two sides of a coin. The first is that wonderful word *grace*. I first got to know it when as a child we always said grace before our meals; that is, either Mom or Dad or one of us children would be asked to thank God for our food. It was to remind our family—and others around the table—that the food before us was a gift. We didn't deserve it, but since it was there we said grace and by so doing served up the reminder that "what we are about to receive" is by God's grace.

In his magnificent book *What's So Amazing About Grace*, Philip Yancey describes grace this way: "Grace means there is nothing we can do to make God love us more—no amount of spiritual calisthenics and renunciations, no amount of knowledge gained from seminaries and divinity schools, no amount of crusading on behalf of righteous causes. And grace means there is nothing we can do to make God love us less—no amount of racism or pride or pornography or adultery or even murder. Grace means that God already loves us as much as an infinite God can possibly love.[53]

Time after time Jesus showed tenderness to people whom the religious establishment ignored, demeaned or rejected. A prostitute became the focus of his attention. A blind man, outside of social considerations or concern, continued to call for Jesus, even to the annoyance of the disciples. Jesus turned to him with healing. A woman unclean by a blood disorder and shunned by the religious establishment (her affliction would force them to go through the elaborate and time-consuming process of ritual cleansing) caught Jesus' attention. She, too, found healing. Jesus' life-enhancing forgiveness looks past what others see—or don't see—bringing into our broken hearts the healing stuff of grace.

In receiving grace, C.S. Lewis, in his sermon called "The Weight of Glory," said, "Indeed, if we consider the unblushing promises of reward and the staggering nature of the rewards promised in the Gospels, it would seem that Our Lord finds our desires, not too strong, but too weak. We are half-hearted creatures, fooling about with drink and sex and ambition when infinite joy is offered us, like an ignorant child who wants to go on making mud pies in a slum because he cannot imagine what is meant by the offer of a holiday at the sea. We are far too easily pleased.[54]

Grace is one of those "staggering rewards."

MERCY—NOT RECEIVING THE PUNISHMENT I DESERVE

The second side of the coin of rebirth is mercy.

In the larger sense, what do I deserve? Do I deserve to live in an eternity of peace and freedom? I'm not a criminal as defined by the Criminal Code; however, in Jesus' view I am, for I've hated a person. That from an eternal perspective, is the same as committing murder. So here I am free as a citizen, but can I expect the same within the courts of the Creator? On what basis within the framework of God's justice am I declared without guilt? On the basis of mercy, which means I've been given an exclusion from the penalty I should get.

The Scriptures make it clear: I've inherited human nature, which is self-centered, choosing to serve my interests rather than God's. (Those who suggest that human nature is good from birth onward may not have raised children!) As lovely as children may be, they are flawed. They will be trained to control their impulses, modify their behavior and hopefully become pleasant and caring. But rooted in our nature is a will that pulls us away from the Creator. For anyone not to get what they deserve, they need to receive mercy.

LOVE

Rabbi Mayer lived in Germany in the eleventh century. He was confined in what then was called an insane asylum. This rabbi was anything but insane. In 1096 he wrote a Jewish verse that forms the core of one of the most beloved Christian songs of the twentieth century. Out of his memory and personal experience of hate and genocide, this Jewish man saw at the core of his existence a God whose love was so vast and deep that it was beyond definition. He penciled on his wall:

> Could we with ink the ocean fill
> And were the skies of parchment made,
> Were ev'ry stalk on earth a quill,
> And ev'ry man a scribe by trade,
> To write the love of God above
> Would drain the ocean dry,
> Nor could the scroll contain the whole
> Tho stretched from sky to sky.

Inspired by this verse, Frederick Lehman, wrote what we now sing:

> The love of God is greater far
> Than tongue or pen can ever tell,
> It goes beyond the highest star
> And reaches to the lowest hell;
> The guilty pair, bowed down with care,
> God gave His Son to win;
> His erring child He reconciled
> And pardoned from his sin.
>
> When years of time shall pass away
> And earthly thrones and kingdoms fall,
> When men, who here refuse to pray,
> On rocks and hills and mountains call,
> God's love so sure shall still endure,
> All measureless and strong;
> Redeeming grace to Adam's race—
> The saints' and angels' song.[55]

What is significant is how God both showed his love and lived his love. When entering the Manger Square in Bethlehem, one is reminded of the frailty of this strip of land on the eastern shore of the Mediterranean, both today and some two thousand years ago. What strikes me most, however, is its physicality. Lily and I took a short walk from the manger location and sat under an outcropping of rock that has served for centuries as a protection for shepherds and sheep. The birth of Jesus is not a fabrication. In real time and in a real place, his birth occurred.

That's what's unique: Jesus was earthly, in that his life came from the impregnation of the young unmarried virgin Mary. Jesus' genesis, the sperm that fertilized the egg, is what makes this without parallel: God the Creator was responsible. The result? Jesus is both God-Creator and God-Human. Forever the divine is fused with the created—the human—and in Jesus the Messiah-Christ, he lives in his cosmic kingdom as the Eternal One.

This means that during his life on this planet, Jesus' life was real. Carving a toy boat in his father's workshop, he bled when the knife slipped. When ridiculed by boyhood friends for being born before his parents were married, he felt social and inner pain. He was real and human. So today, though no longer confined to human dimensions, Jesus by his collective experience knows what we feel. He is not just the Creator who knows all my sides, he knows what it's like to be me. I particularly appreciate Dorothy Sayers' colorful perspective:

> For whatever reason God chose to make man as he is—limited and suffering and subject to sorrows and earth—he had the honesty and courage to take his own medicine. Whatever game he is playing with his creation, he has kept his own rules and played fair. He can exact nothing from man that he has not exacted from himself. He has himself gone through the whole of human experience, from the trivial irritations of family life and the cramping restrictions of hard work and lack of money to the worst horrors of pain and humiliation, defeat, despair, and death. When he was a man, he played the man.

He was born in poverty and died in disgrace and thought it well worthwhile.[56]

Love goes beyond today's sentimentality and finds a new center in costly giving. This is the love that comes our way by God's gift of healing.

THE SOURCE OF NEW BIRTH

We are offered the gift of new life. But where does it come from, and how does it come about?

It comes from above. We use the spatial metaphor "from above," not because God is literally above, but rather because he is beyond the curtain of our knowledge. It means God is not within creation. Ancient religions and current New Age forms of spirituality assume that God is part of the earth and sky. Thus to find God, so the reasoning goes, one searches for him within the rain forest, for example, and within ourselves and other people. There are two important distinctions to be made between the Christian faith and other forms of spirituality.

First, creation comes from the work and ordering of God. Creation is an extension of the Creator. It is not the Creator. Creation is a gift and work of God who after completing it declared it was good. If God is within—synonymous with and part of the created—we are trapped in this human reality infected with rebellion with no source to which we can turn. Planet Earth was afflicted when our original parents rejected the boundaries set out by the Creator. So today this world in which we have been incubated is also afflicted. The trap of equating the creation with the Creator leaves us nowhere we can go but back to ourselves. When asked if he believed in the divine person of Christ, Peter the disciple replied, "If I don't, where else can I turn to for eternal life"

Second, though God brought all of life into existence, this promise of new life is about God bringing his eternal force into our lives. Of all the distinctions between Christianity and other world faiths, this is one of the most critical. The Apostle Paul uses an apt metaphor: our bodies become a temple in which God chooses to live. So from outside of this creation, the Creator-God makes our lives—our body, mind and spirit—his habitation. It is this presence that gives substance to the rebirth.

This new life also comes to us when we face dying. Issues such as this are often ignored until it's too late. Answers don't come by glibly calling out to God. When I asked Major General Louis MacKenzie, of the Canadian Army, about the level of spiritual interest among his soldiers, he said, "It is in direct proportion to the distance to the front line. The closer they get, the more they think about eternity and their spiritual needs."

Though such battle-front faith is to be taken seriously, in many ways it is also trite. Yes, their "God-if-you'll-help-me-now" prayers erupt from deeply felt needs, yet for most there's no serious intent to continue that search if and when they get back home or even to camp. Though fox holes have few atheists, they also have few serious searchers.

If you desire change, it requires a willingness to forgo your past life for this new life. It calls us to set aside our agendas, biases and self-directed goals. And that is a price most of us are not willing to pay. Change is for those who are prepared to risk the adventure.

New life comes to us when we have nothing to offer. It comes when we know we need it. To be self-reliant and self-sufficient is good and admirable. The whole process of growing up is learning how to become a responsible adult, to be able to take care of ourselves. The downside is that we assume self-reliance and self-sufficiency are what make us strong, sometimes to the point of believing we don't need anyone else.

We like to feel that we are in control and that, if we do need help, at least we have some sort of bargaining power with God: "Look, I know I need your help, but I've got this to offer, so how about a trade?" With God it's all or nothing.

Humanism at its core is pride, denying a need for God. Scientific advances create the impression that we got here on our own. This keeps us from falling on our faces before God, admitting we're in need. We view such theatrics as demeaning. They may be, but there is no other way to come and receive the new life offered, except to acknowledge our desperate need.

Is it fair of God to wait until we're in such a position of hurting to make himself available? Margaret Powers wrote the famous poem *Footprints* in which she describes how he has been there all along:

> One night I dreamed a dream.
> I was walking along the beach with my Lord.
> Across the dark sky flashed scenes from my life.
> For each scene, I noticed two sets of footprints in the sand,
> one belonging to me and one to my Lord.
> When the last scene of my life shot before me
> I looked back at the footprints in the sand
> and to my surprise,
> I noticed that many times along the path of my life
> there was only one set of footprints.
> I realized that this was at the lowest
> and saddest times of my life.
> This always bothered me
> and I questioned the Lord
> about my dilemma.
> "Lord, you told me when I decided to follow You,
> You would walk and talk with me all the way.
> But I'm aware that during the most troublesome
> times of my life there is only one set of footprints.
> I just don't understand why, when I needed You most,
> You leave me."
> He whispered, "My precious child,
> I love you and will never leave you
> never, ever, during your trials and testings.
> When you saw only one set of footprints
> it was then that I carried you."[57]

I suspect the reason why we don't hear God's voice or sense his presence is that we aren't listening or looking. Often God is reduced to one among many or as merely an expletive to express contempt or frustration. When we abuse the notion of God by indiscreet language, when we blame God for all sorts of things or when we ignore God's claims on our families, what gives us either the inclination or desire to watch for his footprints, listen to his call or feel his loving touch?

As Dr. Paul Brand describes, in our hurt when the megaphone of life blasts out its cacophony of discordant noise, do we notice how desperate we really are? Listen to the noise raised by your need. Hear and acknowledge it.

A GIFT FOREVER

The day Jesus announced to the public his calling and mission, he did it in his hometown of Nazareth, in the synagogue before his neighbors and religious leaders. As a rabbi he was allowed to link Old Testament texts and offer his comments. For this crowd, who believed they were the only race God cared about, Jesus upset the apple cart. He chose a story from their past to remind them of God's gift to a widow of another ethnic group who had no right to expect this God of the Hebrews to help her.

Elijah the prophet, pursued by Ahab, the king of Israel, was hungry. He met a widow in Sidon and asked her for food. She replied, "I don't have any bread—only a handful of flour in a jar and a little oil in a jug. I am gathering a few sticks to take home and make a meal for myself and my son, that we may eat it—and die."

The prophet promised that if she would make him a meal, the jug of oil would not run dry. She took him at his word, and after making a meal for Elijah, turned to make one for herself and her son. Day after day she went back to the jug for oil, and there was always enough.

That is a metaphor for the gift of life. There is no end to its supply.

Eleven

ENCOUNTERING INNER CHANGE ALONG THE WAY

Let me outline some points to help you along the journey of healing. It begins each morning when we wake and is as relentless as the rising sun. There are no easy shortcuts. Indeed one of the important aspects of this journey is not just arriving but the process of getting there. We needn't concern ourselves with what we'll meet at the end of the journey. That's looked after by Christ; it's in his hands, and we'll happily leave it there. Our calling is to make each day an important moment in the journey so that our steps add to our own wellbeing and take us from the tragedies of life into his healing.

I recommend three aids to assist you on the path:

- link into a Christian community,
- give time for devotions each day, and
- connect with those whose lives express hope, faith and love.

LINKING INTO A CHRISTIAN COMMUNITY

Linking into a Christian community is vital, for we are made to be in community. The stark, individualist thinking of the Western world runs up against the fact that as God's creation we are in need of being with others in faith. The genius of the church in community is that it provides a place where people, regardless of their age, economic wellbeing, education, gender or social standing, are welcomed into the body of Christ. Paul uses this analogy of the body of Christ to help us understand that we are part of Christ's work on earth. Being part of his life-giving community provides one with ingredients essential to our wellbeing.

If you have a place of fellowship and worship, be careful that the accompanying malaise doesn't keep you from attending. Discomfort in having to respond to questions such as "How are you feeling?" or shyness in being noticed if your sorrow is the result of that which is quite public should not keep you from being part of an active Christian church. The nature of community is at the very heart of our social need.

DEVELOPING A TIME FOR DEVOTIONS

Developing a time for devotions is a challenge. Some will find it easier than others, but regardless of the ease with which it becomes a part of your daily life, the life lived in Christ takes special effort to nurture. There are three components to devotions: prayer, Bible reading and devotional reflections. They are all essential to our spiritual health. In my discussions with my medical-scientist brother Cal, he described how the immune system goes through what is called "recapitulating ontogeny." The immune system needs to be reborn; that is, it requires a reorientation so that the good we would have rejected, we now see as self. When Jesus told Nicodemus he had to be remade so his spiritual self would recognize and accept what up to that time was foreign to him, he was calling this learned rabbi into a new life. Once that new life comes, it needs to be fed.

New interior life needs high energy for it to grow and become strong. Given that this is a spiritual new life, it's logical that what it needs is spiritual nurture. As well, following my brother's comparison of the immune system with that of our spirit, the newborn needs the milk of the mother to build up resistance and develop its understanding of self.

Prayer, Bible reading and reflections are the "food" needed for growing new life and giving it understanding of what is good and true, as well as learning what is not.

PRAYER AND BIBLE READING

In our scientific age, the role of prayer as instrumental to our well-being has often been discounted, relegated to the category of snake charmers and faith healers. But that attitude is being challenged. More people recognize that faith can and does make a difference in healing. In *The Faith Factor—Proof of the Healing Power of Prayer*, medical doctor Dale E. Matthews analyzes current scientific studies that show with amazing clarity the role faith has in the healing process. He writes:

> Researchers who have established the faith factor's benefits to health have forged ahead in spite of opposition, saying that the health of one's patients is more important than the health of one's career. We are using the scientific method to prove that the medical effects of religion are not just a matter of faith, but a matter of science. . . . It is entirely possible that, a century from now, people will look back at twentieth-century medicine and say, "Can you believe that those doctors never prayed with their patients? Just think how many lives could have been saved—if only they had set up intercessory-prayer teams in every hospital as we do today!" Will they be as stunned then that we didn't pray for our patients as we would today if doctors didn't wash their hands before treating patients' wounds?[58]

For those with a history and tradition in Bible reading and prayer, you may want to experiment with other forms. If you have no experience, preference or pattern, this can be a very exciting moment. I suggest the following for both prayer and Bible reading:

1. Find a time each day that suits your schedule. It may be early in the morning, before your household is up. You may want to ignore the morning paper. When I pick up the paper, I tend to get distracted and find my prayer and reading time is gone before I know it.
2. Find a place you'll use every day, a setting that becomes associated

with this moment in the day. It may be a favorite chair—stay away from the television—or in some secluded spot of the house.

3. Begin with about fifteen minutes. Don't assume you will automatically be strong in this area. Devotional life is like a muscle, the more you use it the stronger it will get.

4. Avoid trying to be only spontaneous. This will work for the first few days, but you'll find that it becomes boring. Use a guide or outline.

Suggested Formats for Prayer

There are many possible guidelines for praying. Here are some ideas:

A. Read the prayers of others. There are many books with rich prayers that will lift your spirit and bring you into spiritual communion. Don't rely on these exclusively, but they are valuable in providing focus. I especially suggest this to those who are used to an extemporaneous type of praying. When we pray this way, we often get caught in a rut of resorting to the same words and ideas. Reading the prayers of others enriches your thoughts, vocabulary and approaches to praying.

B. Write out some of your prayers. Over the years I've written out my prayers in free verse. While they aren't prayers I'd publish, writing them helps me see what I've said or asked of the Lord.

C. For some years I've used a simple format for praying, not original with me but most helpful. Often I'll set out my watch and divide the time I have to pray in four. I find that even when praying publicly, I will use this as a handy device to keep myself on track. It's called A.C.T.S., an acronym for adoration, confession, thanksgiving and supplication. This pattern has been particularly valuable because it leads me from an important point of departure through the essential ingredients to the conclusion. Here is a brief outline of what might be included in each of these quadrants:

Adoration: We begin with adoring God. The primary focus of adoration is to get our mind into the "space" of God. In this first section we should avoid thanking God for his many provisions. That will come under the third quadrant. The metaphor I try to hold here is of God, who in his infinite power, majesty and love, exists apart from me and creation.

Confession: After seeing my life from the perspective of God's majesty, I can better understand the real issues that need confessing. The picture I have in mind is looking down on a body of water. If I'm in a boat looking over the side, it's difficult to see deep into the water. However, at 500 feet above the surface, I can see further down in the water than when I'm looking from the boat. When I begin with adoration, I see my own needs and sins much better from God's perspective. It is then I can more openly tell God my failures and open my heart to his love and forgiveness.

Thanksgiving: After seeing God in his greatness and following my confession, I am free to express my thanks for all that has come my way. I find a list is helpful, one I can add to as things come to mind during the day.

Supplication: Here I give God my shopping list of issues, needs and problems for which I need his help. We should not feel uncomfortable about such a list. Jesus told the story of a person who was importune; that is, persistent. Because someone had come to his house unexpectedly and he had no food to offer—an embarrassing situation in Middle East culture—he banged on the door of his neighbors until they got out of bed and helped him. The message is, Don't get tired of banging on God's door.

D. I have found that praying some Old Testament verses is a marvelous format for prayer. I'll take a chapter or a few verses and simply read a line and then offer a prayer. For example, here is Psalm 6. It has ten verses, each having a separate thought. Read one verse and then say a prayer that emerges from the idea of that verse.

1. O LORD, do not rebuke me in your anger or discipline me in your wrath.
2. Be merciful to me, LORD, for I am faint; O LORD, heal me, for my bones are in agony.
3. My soul is in anguish. How long, O LORD, how long?
4. Turn, O LORD, and deliver me; save me because of your unfailing love.
5. No one remembers you when he is dead. Who praises you from the grave?
6. I am worn out from groaning; all night long I flood my bed with weeping and drench my couch with tears.

7. My eyes grow weak with sorrow; they fail because of all my foes.
8. Away from me, all you who do evil, for the LORD has heard my weeping.
9. The LORD has heard my cry for mercy; the LORD accepts my prayer.
10. All my enemies will be ashamed and dismayed; they will turn back in sudden disgrace.

Suggestions for Bible Reading

As with prayers, there are many books that can help you by providing a structure for Bible reading with guidelines that can help keep you from being bored or confused. Depending on your familiarity with the Bible, you will want to begin daily reading carefully. Overcommitting yourself to read and study more than you are able can lead to discouragement. So give yourself time to build up a knowledge of the Scriptures.

There are many ways to approach Bible reading. I suggest the following five:

A. Pray promises from the Bible.
Read a promise and then use it as a prayer, asking God to fulfill the promise. Here are ten examples.
1. For the LORD God is a sun and a shield; the LORD bestows favor and honor; no good thing does he withhold from those whose walk is blameless (Ps. 84:11).
2. The LORD is with me; I will not be afraid. What can man do to me? (Ps. 118:6).
3. The LORD is near to all who call on him, in truth. He fulfills the desires of those who fear him; he hears their cry and saves them (Ps. 145:18–19).
4. Trust in the LORD with all your heart and lean not on your own understanding; in all your ways acknowledge him, and he will make your paths straight (Prov. 3:5–6).
5. He gives strength to the weary and increases the power of the weak (Is. 40:29).
6. Those who hope in the LORD will renew their strength. They will soar on wings like eagles; they will run and not grow weary, they will walk and not faint (Is. 40:31).

7. When you pass through the waters, I will be with you; and when you pass through the rivers, they will not sweep over you. When you walk through the fire, you will not be burned; the flames will not set you ablaze (Is. 43:2).

8. With God all things are possible (Matt. 19:26, NIV).

9. For God so loved the world that he gave his one and only Son, that whoever believes in him shall not perish but have eternal life (Jn. 3:16, NIV).

10. For I am convinced that neither death nor life, neither angels nor demons, neither the present nor the future, nor any powers, neither height nor depth, nor anything else in all creation, will be able to separate us from the love of God that is in Christ Jesus our Lord (Rom. 8:38–39, NIV).

B. Use a daily devotional guide. There are many of these; however, it seems that the British are better at writing these guides than others. They usually begin with a verse which you should read, then follow through on the thought that emerges out of that verse. "Daily Bread" is a popular guide.

C. Read until something leaps out at you. Simply take a book of the Bible and read slowly until some idea breaks out. Stop, go back, and read the idea or phrase again so that it's read within the larger context of the chapter. Don't go any further, but write this thought on a note pad. Then take that thought, commit it in prayer, and hold on to it. Henri Nouwen had a habit of finding a thought and then mentally hanging it like a picture on the wall of his mind. He'd stop periodically during the day, and in his mind look up at the promise and thank God for it.

D. Read with a study guide. Bible reading is more of a study than a devotion. While the purpose of a devotional period is to encourage you for the day, if you have a longer period of time for your devotions, and you have up to twenty minutes for Bible reading, then you may want to study a book or a Bible character. It is always helpful to have a note pad for your own ideas, unless you have a study book that gives you room for your own notes.

E. Read through the Bible in a set period of time. There are study Bibles that help you sort out what you need to read in a year, for example. However, unless you are quite familiar with the Bible, I'd recommend you not use this approach at first.

REFLECTIVE READING

No matter what our level of interest and ability in reading, when we feel the effects of hurt and sorrow, we can be lifted by the writings of people who have gone through some of the same struggles as we have and of others who, from the rich repository of experience and insight, can offer healing thoughts.

Here are some suggestions:

Devotional Life

Richard J. Foster has written two classics—*Celebration of Discipline: The Path to Spiritual Growth* and *Freedom of Simplicity*—that, in my view, are pivotal to one's daily devotions. He doesn't tell you how to do your devotions, but gives you the context for their value and purpose. Both books are published by HarperCollins.

Reflection

Henri Nouwen has been one of the most gifted writers of the past few decades. His books have crossed church lines and powerfully touched lives. Among the many he has written, you may want to read *The Wounded Healer* and *A Cry for Mercy*. Most of his books have been published by Doubleday. As well, I recommend *The Broken Body—Journey to Wholeness* by Jean Vanier (Paulist Press).

Pain and Suffering

The classic book on this subject is C.S. Lewis', *The Problem of Pain* (Fount). Three more contemporary books are *Where Is God When It Hurts?* by Philip Yancey (Zondervan Publishing); *Making Sense Out Of Suffering* by Peter Kreeft (Servant Books); and *Can God Be Trusted?* by John G. Stackhouse (Oxford University Press).

FINALLY, CONNECT WITH THOSE WHOSE LIFE EXPRESSES HOPE, FAITH AND LOVE

Hurt and sorrow will deplete your energy, leaving you feeling low and uninspired. Don't stay there. Find opportunities to give and to receive. There is a maxim I've come to appreciate: When feeling tired, exercise, for the very act of expending energy creates energy.

Dave and Evelyn Stiller continue to live this way. When someone is in need, Evelyn is there to love and encourage. From losing her only daughter, Evelyn found that when she made herself available to others and refused to be trapped in her own sorrow, she became a beneficiary.

The same has been true for David. Be it in his leadership in relief and development issues worldwide, or in his home community, he too has learned the principle that we receive when we give away.

Let the Sea of Galilee be a lingering metaphor to give you hope. Resist the deadness of the sea to the south which only takes and never gives.

Finally, may your lasting image be that of Jesus of Nazareth, who from his wounds heals. As you walk this three-fold path to healing, allow hope to open your vision of life and let faith inspire risk so that the loving presence of Christ will bring healing to your hurt.

I would like to hear your story of hope and faith. Please write or email me. What you write will be held in confidence.

Brian C. Stiller
25 Ballyconnor Court
Toronto, Ontario, Canada
M2M 4B3
Email: bstiller@tyndale-canada.edu

ENDNOTES

1. Charles Swindoll, *Hope Again* (Dallas, Texas: Word Publishing, 1996), xi–xii.
2. Viktor E. Frankl, *Man's Search for Meaning* (New York: Pocket Books, 1984), 95.
3. Ibid., 97.
4. Cited in Peter Kreeft, *Making Sense out of Suffering* (Ann Arbor, Michigan: Servant Books, 1986), 109–110.
5. Malcolm Muggeridge, *Twentieth Century Testimony* (Nashville: Thomas Nelson, 1988), 18, 19.
6. Gerald L. Sittser, *A Grace Disguised* (Grand Rapids, Michigan: Zondervan, 1995), 54.
7. Scott Peck, *The Road Less Traveled* (New York: A Touchstone Book, Simon and Schuster, 1978), 91–92.
8. Kenneth E. Bailey, *Poet and Peasant* (Grand Rapids, Michigan: William B. Eerdmans Publishing Company, 1979), 178.
9. Viktor E. Frankl, *The Will to Meaning* (New York: New American Library, 1969), 19.
10. Ibid., 55.
11. Wilma Derksen, *Have You Seen Candace?* (Wheaton, Illinois: Tyndale House Publishers, 1991), 211.
12. Nicholas Wolterstorff, *Lament for a Son* (Grand Rapids, Michigan: William B. Eerdmans, 1987), 23.
13. Ibid., 102.
14. Cited in Philip Yancey, *Where Is God When It Hurts?* (Grand Rapids, Michigan: Zondervan, 1990), 151.
15. Calvin R. Stiller with Brian C. Stiller, *Lifegifts* (Toronto: Stoddart, 1990), 54–59.
16. Sokreaksa "Reaksa" Himm, *The Tears of My Soul* (unpublished manuscript, Toronto, 1998).
17. Cited in C. Stephen Evans, *Despair: A Moment or a Way of Life?* (Downers Grove, Illinois: Inter-Varsity Press, 1973), 13.
18. Cited in M. Harrington, *The Politics at God's Funeral* (New York: Fawcett Crest, 1984), 85.
19. Ibid., 85.
20. Elie Wiesel, *Night* (Toronto: Bantam Books, 1992), 32.
21. Ibid., ix.
22. Evans, 17.
23. Jean-Paul Sartre, *Nausea* (New York: New Directions, 1959), 57.
24. Ibid., 151.
25. Evans, 36.
26. Yancey, *Where Is God?*, 46.

27. C.S. Lewis, *The Problem of Pain* (Fount, 1970), 74.
28. Cited in John G. Stackhouse, Jr., *Can God Be Trusted?* (New York: Oxford University Press, 1998), 77.
29. Ibid., 71.
30. Ibid., 76–78.
31. Ibid., 79.
32. Ibid., 79.
33. Yancey, *Where Is God?*, 95.
34. Cited in James Houston, *In Search of Happiness* (Oxford: A Lion Book, 1990), 31.
35. Ibid., 11.
36. Earl F. Palmer, *The Enormous Exception* (Waco, Texas: Word Books, 1986), 22.
37. Houston, 220.
38. Ibid., 222.
39. Frankl, *Man's Search For Meaning*, 17.
40. Dietrich Bonhoeffer, *The Cost of Discipleship* (New York: Macmillan Publishing Company), 20–21.
41. Frankl, *Man's Search For Meaning*, 86.
42. Stephen Covey, 1998 Calendar, August 20.
43. Ibid., May 16/17.
44. Houston, 61.
45. Ibid., 65.
46. H. Norman Wright, *Resilience* (Ann Arbor, Michigan: Vine Books, 1997), 28.
47. John Powell, *The Christian Vision: The Truth That Sets Us Free* (Allen, Texas: Thomas More, 1984), 123.
48. Himm, 104-106.
49. Cited in Houston, 244.
50. Ibid., 244.
51. Yancey, *Where Is God?*, 209.
52. Johnny Lee Clary, "The Dragon and the Preacher," *Guideposts*, (Sept. 1998): 2–5.
53. Philip Yancey, *What's So Amazing About Grace?* (Grand Rapids, Michigan: Zondervan, 1997), 70.
54. Cited in Houston, 264.
55. Henry Gariepy, *Songs in the Night* (Grand Rapids, Michigan: William B. Eerdmans, 1996), 52.
56. Cited in Yancey, *Where Is God?*, 225.
57. Margaret Fishback Powers, *Life's Little Inspiration Book* (Toronto: HarperCollins, 1995), Introduction.
58. Dale E. Matthews, *The Faith Factor—Proof of the Healing Power of Prayer* (New York: Viking, 1998), 58.